The Measurement of Behavior:
Behavior Modification

Managing Behavior Series

The Measurement of Behavior:
Behavior Modification

THIRD EDITION

Ron Van Houten
and
R. Vance Hall

pro·ed
An International Publisher

8700 Shoal Creek Boulevard
Austin, Texas 78757-6897
800/897-3202 Fax 800/397-7633
www.proedinc.com

© 2001, 1983 by PRO-ED, Inc.
8700 Shoal Creek Boulevard
Austin, Texas 78757-6897
800/897-3202   Fax 800/397-7633
www.proedinc.com

Library of Congress Cataloging-in-Publication Data

Van Houten, Ron.
    The measurement of behavior : behavior modification / Ron Van Houten, R.
Vance Hall.—2nd ed.
        p.   cm.
    Includes bibliographical references.
    ISBN-13: 978-089079861-4 (alk. paper)
    ISBN-10: 0-89079-861-3 (alk. paper)
        1. Behavior modification. 2. Behavioral assessment.   I. Hall, R. Vance
(Robert Vance), 1928-II. Title
BF637.B4 V37 2001
153.8'5-dc21   00-059094
                                                                                              CIP

This book is designed in Palatino and Frutiger.

Printed in the United States of America

        7   8   9   1 0   11

Contents

Foreword

In the 30 years since the publication of the first edition of *The Measurement of Behavior: Behavior Modification* thousands of college students, parents, teachers, managers, and others have learned how to measure human behavior with the help of that work. The book has been used in college classrooms, institutions, workshops, parent training groups, in-service training programs, and other settings in which interested persons gather to learn to use behavior management. The original edition of *The Measurement of Behavior: Behavior Modification* is a classic in the field.

We are proud to bring to the practice of behavior management the third edition of the *The Measurement of Behavior: Behavior Modification.* Ron Van Houten of Mount Saint Vincent University in Halifax, Nova Scotia, a leading behavioral researcher who has conducted successful programs in education, safety research, clinical research, and developmental disabilities, has prepared the third edition. The revised version is updated and expanded to make it an even more complete guide to the measurement of human behavior.

The many practitioners of behavior management throughout the world, and students who are just learning the basics of applied behavior analysis, will find this new edition packed with useful information from the original version and supplemented by treatments of advances in the field. It remains a clear and functional tool.

Because modern behavioral research depends upon keen observation, precise measurement, and effective research designs, it is necessary for behavior analysts to understand these aspects as they study human behavior. The behavior manager must understand and be able to use measurement procedures to apply behavior analysis techniques in the classroom, at home, and on the job.

R. Vance Hall

Introduction

Behavior modification is rooted in learning theory, which in turn is based on the work of such scientists as B. F. Skinner and Ivan Pavlov. Their discoveries depended on keen observation and precise measurement of behavior. In fact, these scientists' most significant contribution to psychology and education is not their definitions of principles, but their development of ways to measure and record observable behaviors. Measurement is central to the behavioral approach because it is the first step in solving a problem. Developing a valid measurement system is like shining a light on a problem because it enables you to clearly see if your efforts bear fruit. People in all walks of life are hoping to influence and change behavior. Without tools for measuring progress, it is difficult for them to move ahead.

Applied behavior analysis has also contributed powerful and practical research methods to enable behavior analysts to test and evaluate the success of their programs. These designs are not based on a multivariate statistical approach but on the traditional scientific method of replication. These powerful designs are well suited for conducting research in applied settings in education, business, medicine, recreation, and government. These designs can also be adapted to provide useful information on the causes of behavior as well as quickly determining effects and side effects of behaviors. The years to come will see their applications in new and exciting areas.

Why Measure Behavior?

Behavior analysis is a pragmatic and practical method for changing behavior. The first step is to carefully define and measure the behavior one wishes to change. Unless the behavior is carefully measured and graphed, it is not possible to see gradual improvements. Persons are easily distracted and have short memories for the details of behavior. For example, even if teachers or employers remember how many times a particular behavior occurred the preceding day, they have difficulty remembering how many times the behavior occurred 6 or 7 days before. Yet, in order to know how well a new program is working, it is necessary to compare how often a behavior occurred before the program was introduced to how often it occurs after the program was introduced. To make matters more complex, some behaviors vary from day to day. That is why behavior analysts must know whether the good and bad days following the introduction of a program are better or worse than the good and bad days before it was introduced.

It is important to measure behavior so that teachers, employers, parents, urban planners, coaches, and others can evaluate how well their programs work. When analysts measure behavior they are holding themselves accountable. If a program does not work, the analyst needs to consider changing his or her approach to the problem. Recorded data also provide excellent sources of feedback to students, employees, children, spouses, and the general public. In many cases, simply providing persons with good feedback about their performance leads to improvements in behavior.

It can also be argued that our understanding of a problem and its causes increases in precision when we can define and measure it. To reliably measure a behavior, a workable and reliable definition is required. Therefore, efforts are made to define the behavior to increase the clarity of our thinking about the problem. Finally, measurement is a prerequisite for a functional analysis, which is a useful way of determining the factors maintaining a problem.

Because modern behavioral research depends on keen observation and precise measurement, it is necessary for behavior managers to understand measurement. This background is required to understand operant research. More importantly, the student of behavior analysis must understand and be able to use measurement procedures to apply behavioral techniques in the classroom, at home, or on the job.

Selecting Behaviors To Be Addressed

Before defining behaviors of interest, the goal of the program must be determined. Questions that need to be answered include what behaviors should be increased, what behaviors should be decreased, and in what situations these changes in behavior should occur. When selecting behaviors to be targeted for change, it is important to ask whether the problem would be solved or greatly improved if these behaviors were to change. Often the answer to this question is based on assumptions which may or may not be true. The behavior analyst should ask why a change in a behavior would make a difference. Always remember that if you change the wrong behaviors, you will not get the hoped-for results.

It is also very important to remember that whenever we decide we wish to decrease a behavior, we also need to select a behavior to increase. For example, if you wish to reduce the frequency of dependent behaviors, you will want to increase corresponding independent behaviors. If you wish to decrease aggression, you may wish to increase cooperative behaviors. It is important to select behaviors to increase whenever you attempt to reduce unwanted behaviors because this will lead to a balanced approach. In many cases, reinforcing new behavior may be all that is required to reduce less desirable behavior. In other cases, strengthening behavior that competes with unwanted behavior will make it much easier to bring about a behavior change. Finally, looking for behavior to reinforce helps keep you proactive rather than reactive in your approach to changing behavior. The primary disadvantage of a reactive approach is that it can easily become overly punitive and damage your relationship with the persons you are trying to help.

Defining Behavior

Even the best measurement systems are useless if the behavior of interest is poorly defined. If the definition of the behavior is fuzzy or vague, the observer cannot collect accurate data, regardless of the measurement technique employed. Therefore, the first step in measurement is to accurately and reliably define or pinpoint the behavior in question. In addition, we should deal only with behaviors that are observable and measurable.

Behavior may be sensed by seeing, hearing, tasting, feeling or smelling. We can also observe the measurable products of behavior such as misspelled words in a typed letter, the wreck of an automobile, the amount of litter on a playground, whether the garbage is out by the curb, or whether shipping containers are completely filled.

The key to success is to define the behavior or its product so that little or no subjective evaluation may enter into observation. If the definition requires subjective judgment, no two observers will see the same thing. Therefore a good definition should meet the following three standards (Kazdin, 2000). First, it should be written clearly enough that someone reading it can easily repeat it in his or her own words. If observers cannot state the definition in their own words, then they have only memorized it and do not understand it. By specifying the definition in their own words they are creating the definition. This standard can be met by rewriting the definition until someone else can read it and state it in his or her own words without changing the meaning. Second, the definition should specify the boundary, or edge, of the definition. Many times a definition does not anticipate all the forms the behavior of interest can take. In these cases the definition is incomplete. An incomplete definition can be made complete by discussing new instances and making decisions about how they will be scored. Third, the definition should be objective. To be objective the definition must refer to observable characteristics of behavior.

Writing a Definition

Most persons use broad categories to define behaviors. We often hear words such as neat, messy, cooperative, defiant, and so on. The first step in objectively measuring any behavior is to list specific examples of the behavior. For example, if you are interested in recording a child's messy behavior, you would write down specific behaviors or products of behaviors you call messy. Examples may be leaving clothes around the house, leaving toys on the floor, or leaving smears on furniture or appliances. You should always write the behaviors on a piece of paper so you can revise your definition if you find that it is vague or incomplete. When defining a behavior you should always ask yourself whether it is defined so that someone else can read your definition and then observe the behavior at the same time that you do and record the same thing.

Exercise

What is the first step in defining a general behavior? _____

_____

What are the three standards a good definition should meet?

1. _____

2. _____

3. _____

Give a behavioral definition of a "hyperactive" behavior. Make sure your examples are specific.

_____

_____

_____

_____

(continues)

Give a behavioral definition of "courteous service" at an automobile service center.

_____

_____

_____

_____

Give a behavioral definition of motorists yielding to pedestrians. _____

_____

_____

_____

_____

If you are working through this book with a group of students, compare your answers. Notice the diversity of the behaviors that can cause someone to be labeled hyperactive or aggressive. These differences underscore the need to reach common ground by defining behavior very precisely.

The motorists yielding to pedestrians example shows how a definition needs to be well thought out to be complete. For example, you can score vehicles that stop for the pedestrian or slow enough to allow the pedestrian to cross as yielding, if the pedestrian was standing at the crosswalk and facing the road. Motorists who do not stop or slow to allow the pedestrian to cross would be scored as not yielding. However, it is also necessary to have a criterion for determining whether the person could stop when the pedestrian first appeared. If the motorist was too close to the crosswalk it would not be reasonable to expect the motorist to stop. Therefore, a distance has to be selected that would provide a reasonable stopping distance. Only if the motorist is beyond that point when the pedestrian appears would it be reasonable to score him or her as not yielding. This example shows that it is often necessary to come up with a definition, try it out, and then modify it before it works.

Independent Observers

Comparing the degree to which two persons independently observing the same behavior at the same time have observed the same thing allows us to assess the adequacy of our measurement techniques and how well we have defined or pinpointed the behavior. This is done by calculating interobserver or interscorer agreement. These measures provide a check on the reliability of observational systems and help assess the exactness of the behavioral definition, the appropriateness of the measurement system selected, and the possibility of observer bias.

When two persons observe the same behavior at the same time to check the reliability of the measurement system, it is important that the two observers record or score the behavior independently. Each observer should be unaware of what the other observer is recording. When both observers measure a behavior in this way they are said to be *independent observers.* It is also desirable for the independent second observer to be unaware of the experimental conditions in effect. This helps reduce the possibility of observer bias affecting the results.

If agreement is not obtained between two observers, it typically means one of the following:

1. **There is a problem with the definition.** For example, the definition may not have been clear. If the definition is not clear, both observers may define the behavior differently. It is also possible that the definition is not complete. If the boundaries are not clearly defined, the two observers may be scoring marginal examples of the behaviors differently. Finally, the definition may not be objective. All of these problems can usually be fixed by having the observers discuss what they are doing while they both score the behaviors together until they sort out the problems with the definition.

2. **The task is too complex for the observers.** Sometimes there are too many behaviors to score. This problem can usually be fixed by simplifying the task or providing more training. If the observers are having difficulty with one aspect of the task, they can practice scoring that part alone until they can score it reliably. Another factor that can influence the complexity of the task is the design of the recording sheet. This problem can be fixed by redesigning the sheet so it is easier to use. Examples of ways to simplify the sheets include making sure that related items are located next to each other on the sheet, designing the sheet so it can be filled out with the fewest number of marks, and using icons to make identifying the items more intuitive.

3. **The observation period is too long.** This problem can be fixed by reducing the length of the recording period or by giving observers more frequent rest breaks.

4. **The observers have not received sufficient training.** This problem is fixed by providing more training. Sometimes it helps to provide separate training in scoring a behavior that is particularly difficult to score because the observers' behaviors usually change faster when they are trained in isolation.

5. **One of the observers may be biased.** This problem can typically be fixed by not giving the observers too much information about the purpose of the experiment.

Exercise

What is an independent observer? _____

_____

_____

Name five reasons why observers may have poor interobserver agreement.

1. _____

2. _____

3. _____

4. _____

5. _____

Measurement Techniques

Three methods are commonly used to measure and record behavior: *automatic recording, direct measurement of permanent products,* and *observational recording.*

Automatic Recording

When an individual's behavior activates an electrical or mechanical apparatus which in turn makes a record automatically, we have automatic recording. Automatic recording is used by traffic engineers when they use devices to count traffic, measure the speed of traffic, and measure the number of vehicles waiting to make a turn. Teachers employ automatic recording when they use computers to keep a record of their students' success when they work on computer-assisted instruction. In business, companies in a call center may use computers to track behaviors of interest in their sales force. A trucking company can use automatic recording to measure driver behavior related to safety such as speed, rest breaks, and so on. In the aviation industry, automatic recording is used to record events that occur prior to an accident. In applied research it is sometimes possible to employ automatic recording, and with the microchip revolution we should see greater availability of inexpensive and practical ways of measuring people's behavior automatically.

It is generally most convenient to use automatic recording when the recording device is already present in the environment. For example, if you are interested in changing behaviors to produce a reduction in energy consumption, you could directly measure energy consumption by taking readings off the watt-hour meter present in most homes, businesses, and schools. Similarly, individuals interested in measuring tardiness in a work setting could use a time clock. Other examples of machines that help measure behavior are the radar used by police to measure the speed of vehicles, scales to measure an individual's weight, odometers on cars to measure the number of miles or kilometers driven, pedometers to measure the number of miles or kilometers walked, and turnstiles to measure the number of visitors. Whenever you can use an already-present device to automatically record behaviors in which you are interested, you should do so. The major advantages of devices already present is that they cost little or nothing and save considerable time and effort.

The primary advantages of automatic recording are (a) the precision allowed by automation, (b) the low rate of monitoring or direct supervision required from the researcher, and (c) the easy translation of the automated output into numerical terms. Sometimes the development of a new technology to allow someone to automatically measure a problem goes a long way toward solving the problem. For example, in the medical field many hospital infections and deaths are caused by poor staff hand-washing practices. The development of a device that could measure how well hospital staff washed their hands not only would help researchers to collect objective data on this problem, but also would likely be part of the solution to the problem because the device would be a good basis for providing feedback to staff. For this reason, finding practical and innovative ways to automatically record behavior should be a major goal of behavior analysts.

Unfortunately, it may not always be possible to use automatic recording. The major disadvantages associated with automated recording devices include (a) the expense of the equipment, (b) the skilled personnel required to install and service the equipment, (c) the lack of flexibility or ability to record many specific behaviors, and (d) that some behaviors of interest to parents, teachers, and administrators cannot be recorded with automated equipment. High cost does not always preclude the use of automated equipment. In one study, researchers measured the driving behavior of police with the help of a device called a data logger placed in the trunks of patrol cars. By measuring driving behavior in this way (and applying consequences), administrators were able to reduce damage to police vehicles due to accidents. Savings more than offset the expense of the equipment. In this case, the only practical way to reliably measure the behaviors of interest was expensive but also was time and cost-effective (Larson, Schnelle, Kirchner, Carr, Domash, & Risley, 1980).

Computers can facilitate the automatic measurement of behavior. Many different kinds of behavior can be measured with computers. Examples of behaviors easily recorded by computers are academic responses made to instructional material presented by the computer and the performance of office staff working at computer terminals. With the increasing availability of microcomputers in schools, at work, and in the home, it is possible to measure much human behavior automatically. One advantage of using a computer to measure behavior is that it is possible to look at the resulting data in many different ways. For example, data can be examined in terms of percentage correct, correct rate, error rate, and time spent on task. The computer rapidly makes all the necessary calculations. As computers become more powerful, smaller, and less expensive, they will become even more important in applied behavior analysis. Today they represent a relatively untapped database. For example, a behavior analyst who wishes to promote healthful eating habits through a multifaceted community program could assess the effectiveness of the program by measuring the percentage of healthful foods purchased. Supermarket chains have daily computer records which could easily generate the percentage of fruits, vegetables, whole grains, and other healthful foods sold. With cooperation it is possible to tap into these ongoing databases in order to evaluate program efficacy.

✎ Exercise

_____

What is automatic recording? _____

_____

_____

You are correct if you said it is the automatic recording of behavior by a machine.

Think of examples of machines in your natural environment that can be used to record behavior. (Remember, machines can measure behavior indirectly—for example, a watt-hour meter measures energy use.)

	Type of machine	Behavior it records
1.	_____	_____
2.	_____	_____
3.	_____	_____

Direct Measurement of Permanent or Lasting Products

Academic Behaviors in Schools

Behavior can be measured through the direct observation of lasting products. Many activities result in products that last long enough to be measured and recorded. Teachers frequently observe and measure permanent products that result from behavior of students in the classroom. These include the number of correct words on weekly spelling tests, the number of properly punctuated sentences in a writing lesson, the number of correct words-per-minute on a timed typing drill, the use of perspective in a picture painted during art period, or the percentage of completed papers turned in by a class each day.

Consider the Characteristics of the Material

Direct measurement of lasting products is the best way to measure many academic behaviors. Before beginning to collect data, it is necessary to select the aspect of student performance you wish to measure. One factor that may determine which form of scoring to use is the nature of the material you wish to score. If you are giving weekly tests in a subject area and the length of tests is kept constant, it may be good enough to simply keep track of the number of problems each student works correctly each week. However, if the length of the tests varies each week it is better to score the percentage of each test completed correctly. When the length of an assignment varies it is difficult to know whether an increasing score is the result of the student working harder or of the student being given a longer test. Similarly, if the difficulty of assignments varies too much, it is uncertain whether changes in number completed correctly come about as a result of a change in the student's behavior or as a result of a change in the difficulty of the work. When difficulty is allowed to vary too much, neither the total number correct nor the percentage correct will be an adequate measure.

Consider the Purpose for Recording

Another factor to consider when choosing how to score material is your purpose in recording it. If you are concerned with reducing the number of errors made on weekly tests, you can record the number of errors. If you are interested in speed, then percentage measures or counts will not be as useful as work rate. Work rate is calculated by dividing the number of problems completed by the amount of time spent working them. If you give timed drills on basic number facts ($3 + 4 = $ ___), then you can score the number of problems worked correctly per minute along with the number of problems worked incorrectly per minute. A similar technique is used in scoring timed typing drills. If you are interested in diversity rather than number, accuracy, or speed, you can score the number of different items of a particular type. For example, in one study, researchers were interested in increasing the variety of painting techniques used by preschoolers, therefore they measured the number of different types of strokes the children used (Goetz & Salmonson, 1972).

When selecting the aspect of a behavior you wish to change, pick the aspect that will make the most difference. In general, the largest components are the most important. For example, if a boy is labeled *aggressive* because he frequently threatens other children, then changing this behavior will lead to the greatest increase in satisfaction in those interacting with him. Remember that it is not possible to measure or change all of someone's behavior;

therefore, it is important to carefully choose those aspects of someone's behavior that you wish to measure and change. Always try to get the most improvement with the least amount of effort.

Exercise

What are two things that determine what you score in measuring lasting products?

1. _____

2. _____

You are correct if you said that what you score depends on your purpose for scoring behavior and the nature of the material you are scoring.

Nonacademic School Behaviors

Many nonacademic behaviors produce permanent products that can be measured and recorded. In schools we see such permanent products as writing on desktops, water on the floors or walls of the lavatories, and paper on the playground. The major problem confronting the researcher is how to score these behaviors. Are we concerned with the number of marked desktops, the number of marks on each desktop, whether water is splashed on the floor, how much water is splashed on the floor, and so on? It is often easier to note that you are dealing with a lasting product than it is to figure out how to score it. In the case of water on the lavatory floor, we could score whether or not there is any water on the floor. Unfortunately, this would not be a sensitive measure. Alternatively, we could divide the floor into grids. If the floor is tiled we could count the number of wet tiles each day. Permanent product behavior often comes in discrete chunks, such as the number of school windows broken each week by vandals. Sometimes there are too many products of behavior to measure in this way. For example, it would be difficult to measure litter by counting every piece of litter in a schoolyard each day. A better way would be to divide the schoolyard into grids and record the amount of litter in several randomly selected grids, either by counting the pieces or by weighing the litter. When we are measuring only how much of a product occurs in a randomly selected part of the environment we are using a sampling approach to measure the behavior.

Exercise

When there is too much or too many of a product to conveniently measure, we can make our job easier by

_____

_____

You are correct if you said divide the task and sample the behavior.

Measuring Permanent Products in Other Settings

It is sometimes easy to determine how to score a behavior. In the home we may observe lasting products of behavior by counting the number of articles of clothing left in the living room, by noting whether the dishes have been washed, whether toys have been put away, whether the lights have been turned off, whether a child's hair has been combed, whether the floor has been swept or the beds have been made. Business examples include the number of orders processed per day, the number of keyboarding errors per page, the units of a product produced or shipped, or the number of defective parts manufactured per shift. Community examples include the number of persons parked in more than one space, the number of nonhandicapped persons parked in handicapped spaces, and whether the sidewalks are properly cleared of ice and snow after each storm.

Even when dealing with straightforward examples it is necessary to decide when to measure behavior. For example, if a boy is to make his bed every morning you could check each day after breakfast. If you are recording whether lights have been turned off, you may wish to measure this behavior several times each day at specified times. How much effort you put into recording a behavior will depend on how much you want to change it.

Making a Recording Sheet

Finally, you should have a recording sheet. For example, if you are recording how many lights have been left on that should have been switched off, you could make the rounds, checking rooms every hour. A sheet to record the results of these checks might look like this:

Date	7:00 PM	8:00 PM	9:00 PM	10:00 PM
5/25	1	3	4	3
5/26				
5/27				
5/28				

Each square contains the number of lights left on when no one was in the room. These data could be summarized by calculating the mean number of lights left on each night. When you record depends on the time of day you have a problem. Most often you will need to design some form of checklist to measure the product you have selected.

Exercise

Suggest two other examples of lasting products that could be measured to record the level of specific behavior.

1. _____

2. _____

On a separate sheet of paper, define how and when you would record one of these behaviors, and either draw up a sample recording form or prepare one using a spreadsheet.

Interscorer Agreement (Reliability)

If you are recording a lasting product as part of a research project, you will obtain a measure of interscorer agreement. Interscorer agreement ensures that it is possible to objectively score a product and that there is no bias on the part of the individuals doing the scoring. This may be done by a second person who independently scores the behavior during several sessions (usually a minimum of two sessions during each condition of the study). If you are checking to see whether lights are on, the second observer can check each room several seconds after the first observer. When scoring papers, the second person can rescore the papers after the first person has finished.

Once both persons have scored the behavior, the records are compared. If both observers score the behavior exactly the same, an agreement is counted. If they score a behavior differently, a disagreement is scored. Interscorer agreement is equal to the number of agreements divided by the number of agreements plus the number of disagreements.

$$\text{Interscorer agreement} = \frac{\text{agreements}}{\text{agreements} + \text{disagreements}}$$

$$\text{Percentage interscorer agreement} = \text{interscorer agreement} \times 100$$

In the following example, two observers independently recorded how many lights were left burning in unoccupied rooms. The amount of disagreement would depend upon how well one defined what constituted an unnecessarily burning light.

	7:00	8:00	9:00	10:00	11:00	12:00
Observer 1	2	0	1	0	1	2
Observer 2	2	0	1	1	1	2

At 7:00, 8:00, 9:00, 11:00, and 12:00 P.M. both observers agreed on the number of lights left on unnecessarily. However, at 10:00 they disagreed. Therefore, percentage of interscorer agreement is figured as follows:

$$\frac{\text{agreements}}{\text{agreements} + \text{disagreements}} \times 100 = \frac{5}{5+1} = \frac{5}{6} = 83\%$$

When two persons independently score a student's work, items scored the same by both observers are agreements while items scored differently are disagreements. The percentage of interscorer agreement is computed as in the above example.

Photographic and Video Evidence

It is sometimes possible to make a lasting product more permanent by taking a photograph. For example, in a study on vandalism, photos can be taken of all damage for later study. If you are doing a study on nail-biting, you could photograph fingernails on a regular basis. If this is done from a constant distance and with a ruler next to the fingers, the photos will be very useful. In one study, photos were used to measure the number of different types of constructions preschoolers built each day (Goetz & Baer, 1971). Public libraries routinely use photographic evidence to record who has checked out particular books.

Exercise

List below another product that could be recorded by photography. _____

_____

Another way to score permanent products is to videotape the products and score them at a later date. One advantage of video scoring is that it is possible to rescore additional products from the videotape or disk that you did not identify as important during the study period. Often we think of additional things that would have been useful to measure after the study has been completed or when considering the comments of editors or reviewers. If the products are rescored only in real time, it is impossible to address these concerns without repeating the study.

Review Quiz 1

1. Why is it important to define behaviors carefully?

_____

_____

(continues)

2. To create a good definition, what three standards must be met?

   a. _____

   b. _____

   c. _____

3. Describe a teacher who might be labeled "lazy" in behavioral terms.

   _____

   _____

   _____

4. Why is it necessary to have an independent second observer when carrying out a research study?

   _____

   _____

5. What five things would you look at if interobserver agreement were poor?

   a. _____

   b. _____

   c. _____

   d. _____

   e. _____

6. Give two examples of behaviors that computers can record automatically.

   a. _____

   b. _____

(continues)

7. List four everyday behaviors that can be measured by already-present automatic devices.

   a. _____

   b. _____

   c. _____

   d. _____

8. List two behaviors in each of the following settings that can be measured as permanent products.

   In the classroom:

   a. _____

   b. _____

   In the schoolyard:

   a. _____

   b. _____

   In the home:

   a. _____

   b. _____

   At work:

   a. _____

   b. _____

   In the community:

   a. _____

   b. _____

(continues)

9. In one study, two teachers independently scored a student's answers on a science test. One teacher scored the original test while the second teacher scored a copy of the test. Both teachers scored 10 out of the 12 items the same. They scored the remaining 2 items differently. What is the interscorer agreement percentage on this test?

Observational Recording

When an observer looks at a person's behavior and makes a record of what he or she sees or hears as it occurs, observational recording is taking place. Observational recording can be done live or from audio or video recordings. There are many ways to observe and record behavior as it occurs.

ABC Recording

ABC stands for Antecedent, Behavior, and Consequence. An antecedent is something that occurs before the behavior of interest occurs or fails to occur. The consequence is anything that changes in the environment following the behavior. This could be a change in someone else's behavior or a change in the physical environment. The purpose of this recording method is to identify important behaviors and possible factors that are associated with their occurrence as well as possible consequences that may maintain them. The observer writes down important things as they happen, recording the time as well as relevant information about the situation, such as the setting, who was present, and the type of task or activity taking place. This record is then examined to determine if there is any relationship between events happening before or after a behavior of interest.

This technique allows the recording of many classes of behavior. A disadvantage is that it is impossible to obtain a completely accurate record in most situations because it is usually not possible to record all the details while observing. ABC recording is usually impractical for extended data collection, although an observer may wish to jot down as many behaviors as possible when beginning an observation. This helps identify behaviors he or she may wish to record later using another observational technique. Thus, a running account of the behavior of a child labeled aggressive may reveal that he or she frequently bites and kicks. The observer may then decide to observe biting and kicking behaviors, using a frequency counting procedure to obtain a behavioral record. ABC recording may also provide hints about why someone is engaging in a particular behavior. For example, if a task is usually postponed or stopped following a behavior, the person may be trying to escape that task. If attention usually follows a behavior, the person may be engaging in the behavior to get attention. However, things can get tricky. Is it the attention that is the reinforcer, or is the attention associated with a task being stopped? If it is the latter, the person could be engaging in the behavior to escape that task. This type of question is best addressed by conducting a functional analysis. This topic is addressed later in the book.

 Exercise

Select and record an individual's behavior in a specific situation during a 15-minute period using ABC recording. Try to select several behaviors you believe to be worth further study. Try to identify what factors seem to be associated with the occurrence of these behaviors and changes that occur following these behaviors.

Behavior Counts

One of the most practical and useful recording procedures is frequency counting or event recording. An observer counts the number of discrete events of a certain class of behavior as they occur during a given time. For instance, a teacher may count the number of times a certain pupil participates in class discussion during a 40-minute class period. A parent may tally the number of times per day a son or daughter arrives on time for meals. An employer may count the number of times an employee leaves his work position. It is important to remember to keep the length of the observation time the same each day if you are keeping track of how often a behavior occurs. If you keep observation time constant, calculating rates by dividing the number of times the behavior occurs by the total amount of time becomes unnecessary.

Counting behavior is a simple procedure that usually does not interfere with ongoing tasks. It produces a numerical output that is easy to graph and record. Counting behavior is most useful when the behavior has a clear beginning and end and occurs for a brief time. If the behavior persists for 10 seconds some times and 10 minutes at other times, event recording may lose important information. Frequency counting is most useful when the behavior is very obvious. If a behavior is obvious, as when a child throws a tantrum, hits another child, or asks you a question in class, it is easy to note even when you are busy with other things. However, if the behavior is more subtle (such as two children sharing in a class of 30), it is easy to miss unless you are watching all the time. Furthermore, some behaviors such as being absent from school, taking a nap, or going fishing may lend themselves to counting, but last a long time.

Exercise

Behavior counting (event recording) is most suitable for recording behaviors that:

1. _____

   _____

2. _____

   _____

You understand the use of behavior counting if you answered that (a) the behaviors have a discrete beginning and end, and (b) when the behavior occurs, is difficult to miss.

Keeping a Record

Some teachers, parents, students, supervisors, and others tally (𝓗𝓗 ///) events as they occur, using a handheld computer. Others use a pencil on a note pad or a piece of masking tape on the wrist or on a pupil's desk. It is also possible to use marks on a chalkboard, a golfer's wrist counter, or a supermarket or knitting counter. If you are not using a handheld computer that records the time automatically, it is best to record the time of day the behavior occurs rather than to tally it. This provides additional information and allows you to calculate interobserver agreement in a way that is acceptable to most forums and journals.

A sample recording sheet for event recording is illustrated below.

Date	Time 1	Time 2	Time 3	Time 4	Time 5	Time 6	Time 7
May 1	9:50	10:28	11:51	1:32	1:40	3:00	
May 2	10:25	11:45	1:37	2:30			

If the behavior does not occur too often you need only record the time to the nearest minute. From the sample record above, you can see that a behavior being recorded during the school day occurred six times on May 1 and four times on May 2.

If the behavior occurs several times per minute you can record the time to the nearest second. Behaviors occurring this rapidly require observers to give their undivided attention to recording.

Behaviors that can be recorded in the classroom using frequency or event recording are talk outs, crying, number of pupils late, number of hand raises, and number of correctly enunciated "s" sounds. Behaviors lending themselves to behavior counts in other settings include temper tantrums, number of cars coming to a complete stop at a stop sign, cups of coffee consumed, cigarettes smoked, phone calls received, shots taken during a basketball game, number of positive comments made by a business associate, number of complaints made, and number of absences from work.

Self-Monitoring

Making a record of your own behavior is called self-monitoring. One of the most frequently used methods of self-monitoring is behavior counts, as discussed in the previous section. For example, employers who wish to know how often they give approval and recognition to their employees, or teachers who wish to know how often they praise their students, can record each time they deliver praise or recognition on a counter in their pocket, or they can make a tally on a sheet of paper. It is also useful to record the times of less frequent behaviors. Keeping records of how often you emit a particular behavior is the first step in learning to increase or decrease the frequency of that behavior. Simply recording how often behaviors occur can sometimes lead to an increase in the frequency of behaviors we want to engage in more often, or a decrease in the frequency of behaviors we want to engage in less often. It is also helpful to make notes of what happens before and after a particular behavior. This information is helpful in developing ways to change behavior.

Reliability

Interscorer agreement is calculated by having a second person independently record the behavior during several sessions for each phase of the study. Sound and effective behavior management depends upon reliable measurement procedures. If reliable measurement procedures are not used, it is possible for the behavior to remain stable while the recording of the behavior changes because of observer bias. Conversely, it is possible for the behavior to change while the record remains unchanged.

Interobserver agreement provides added confidence that it is indeed the behavior that has changed from one condition to another. The formula for calculating the percentage of interobserver agreement is the same as for interscorer agreement when scoring permanent products.

When counting behavior, circle on both lists those times appearing on both observers' lists (agreements). Then, add the number of circled times from either list (agreements), divide by the same number plus the number of uncircled times from both lists, and multiply the result by 100 to obtain the percentage of interobserver agreement. The following is an example.

Observer 1	Observer 2
(10:01)	(10:01)
10:15	(11:07)
(11:07)	(12:15)
(12:15)	12:30
(1:00)	(1:00)
(2:15)	(2:15)
(3:40)	(3:40)

$$\text{Percentage interobserver agreement} = \frac{6}{6+2} = \frac{6}{8} = .75 \times 100 = 75\%$$

Exercise

Calculate interobserver agreement in the following example:

Observer 1	Observer 2
9:01	9:01
9:07	9:07
9:16	9:23
9:23	9:24
9:24	9:30
9:30	9:41
9:32	9:43
9:41	10:05
10:04	11:07
11:07	11:46
11:46	11:48
11:48	12:00
12:00	12:05
12:05	

If a simple tally of behaviors is used, the percent of observer agreement is determined by dividing the lower frequency count by the higher frequency count and multiplying by 100, as follows:

	Day 1	Day 2	Day 3	Day 4
Observer One	卌 //	卌 ///	卌 ////	卌 //
Observer Two		卌 /		卌 //

In Day 2, observer agreement was as follows:

$$\frac{\text{lower frequency}}{\text{higher frequency}} = \frac{6}{8} = .75 \times 100 = 75\%$$

What was the agreement on Day 4? _____

Checklists

This is one of the most useful ways to record behavior. To use a checklist, list behaviors and check off whether they occur. To use a checklist to score a behavior, we must classify the behavior according to discrete categories such as performed versus not performed, correct versus incorrect, appropriate versus inappropriate, and so on. Typically, the number of times one has to evaluate the behavior is predetermined. Checklists are useful in measuring safety-related behaviors and are often used at dangerous work sites such as nuclear power plants and the cockpits of airliners. Checklists can also be used by parents, teachers, and employers to measure completion of work-related tasks. Other uses of checklists include measuring numbers of motorists yielding to pedestrians, children cleaning their rooms, students cleaning and organizing their desks, and servers preparing meals in attractive arrangements on plates. Checklists can be used to measure the behavior of one individual or they can be used to measure the behavior of a group. Almost all checklists need to be piloted before they can be used. First the sheet is designed and then it is tried out. If problems are noted, the design of the sheet or the definitions are revised until the sheet can be used for the job for which it is intended.

Duration Recording

It may be more important to know how long a behavior lasts than to know how often it occurs. For instance, a child might suck her thumb only once a day but her thumbsucking might last several hours. Duration recording is used if the elapsed time of a behavior varies over a wide range. A stopwatch or wrist chronograph is the most efficient tool for making duration recordings. It is also possible to use a handheld computer to collect duration data. One advantage offered by this approach is that you can record many durations at the same time. If you do not have a handheld computer or a stopwatch, you can record on a piece of paper the time the behavior begins and the time it ends. When you have finished recording, take the difference between the two times and compute how long the behavior persisted.

Depending on the duration of the behavior, the observer may wish to record it to the nearest second, minute, or quarter hour. In most applied studies, the observer usually records the duration of behavior to the nearest minute. It is also possible to measure exact times using the time code from a videotape viewed on a frame-by-frame basis. Retting and Van Houten (2000) used this approach to measure how much extra time was required for vehicles to enter an intersection after the traffic light turned green before and after the stop line was moved back 16 feet. Measuring the increase in time was important because it could afford some protection from intersection crashes associated with motorists on the cross street that entered the intersection just after the light turned red.

Exercise

Suggest four behaviors for which duration recording can be used.

1. _____

2. _____

3. _____

4. _____

Some examples of correct answers are how much time a worker spends each day in overtime, how long employees spend on coffee breaks, how long a child spends crying after being put to bed, and how long members of a track team spend running each day.

Providing interobserver agreement for duration recording consists of presenting the mean or average difference between the two observers' durations on days that both observers recorded the behavior along with the range of the differences. An example follows.

Date	Observer 1	Observer 2	Difference
Aug 15	23 min	23 min	0 min
Aug 16	32 min	33 min	1 min
Aug 17	5 min	5 min	0 min
Aug 18	8 min		
Aug 19	9 min		
Aug 20	29 min	28 min	1 min
Aug 21	59 min		
Aug 22	60 min	58 min	2 min
Aug 23	78 min		
Aug 24	94 min	94 min	0 min

The average difference between the durations reported by the two observers is equal to the sum of the differences (in this case $0 + 1 + 0 + 1 + 2 + 0 = 4$), divided by the number of times both observers recorded the behavior (6 times). Therefore, the mean or average difference $= \frac{4}{6} = .66$ minutes.

The range of the differences refers to shortest and longest differences, in this case 0 and 2 minutes. Hence, the mean difference is .66 minutes with a range from 0 to 2 minutes.

Exercise

Compute the mean difference and range in the following example.

Session	Observer 1	Observer 2	Difference
1	57 sec	57 sec	_____
2	81 sec	83 sec	_____
3	21 sec		
4	76 sec	76 sec	_____
5	81 sec		
6	89 sec	88 sec	_____
7	91 sec		
8	101 sec	106 sec	_____
9	14 sec		
10	12 sec	11 sec	_____
11	14 sec		
12	8 sec	10 sec	_____
13	21 sec		
14	5 sec	5 sec	_____

Mean difference = _____ sec, with a range of _____ to _____ seconds.

The size of the average difference between the duration reported by two observers depends on several factors. One factor is the timing instruments. If both observers use stopwatches, smaller differences will occur than if they record behavior starts or stops with regular watches or a wall clock. Another factor is how often the behavior starts and stops during a session. If the duration over the session is recorded by starting a stopwatch each time the behavior begins and stopping it each time the behavior ceases, an error may be introduced each time the observers use their stopwatches. One way to deal with this problem is to separately record each duration within the session. The average difference between these durations can then be calculated.

There is no rule of thumb about how much of an average difference is acceptable. A large difference could indicate observer bias, a poorly defined target behavior, or lack of concentration. The difference in the behavior produced by a program should be considerably greater than the average difference between the two observers' reported durations.

Latency Recording

It is sometimes important to know how much time elapses between an event and a behavior. Such a measure is called latency. For example, we might be interested in the time that elapses between a preschool teacher giving an instruction for a child to sit down and when the child sits, a call being received and returned, or a customer arriving and being served. These intervals are latencies. We might also be interested in measuring the time that elapses between when a child is told to clean his room and when this task is completed. Or we might want to know how long it takes a secretary to complete a set amount of assigned keyboarding. Although the interval between an event such as an instruction and the completion of a behavior is not a true latency, it can be considered one for behavior measurement purposes. Latency recording is similar to duration recording because it usually involves using a stopwatch or clock to time an interval. Observers frequently use a recording sheet on which the time of the initial instruction or cue is recorded and the time of the beginning (or the completion) of the behavior is noted. The time that elapses between these points is referred to as the *latency* of the behavior.

Exercise

List two behaviors for which latency is important to observe and measure.

1. _____

2. _____

Interobserver Agreement

Reporting the interobserver agreement of latency data is done in much the same way as duration data except that the mean difference in latency along with the range of differences is reported. An example follows.

Latency Data

Session	Observer 1	Observer 2	Difference
1	14 sec		
2	12 sec	12 sec	0 sec
3	15 sec	17 sec	2 sec
4	6 sec		
5	20 sec	19 sec	1 sec
6	10 sec		

$$\overline{x} \text{ diff} = \frac{0 + 2 + 1}{3} = \frac{3}{3} = 1 \text{ sec}$$

Hence, the mean difference between observers' latencies was 1 second with a range of 0 to 2 seconds.

Interval Recording

Interval recording is used where there are ongoing play or work behaviors. Interval recording requires someone with no other responsibility than to observe and record the behavior of interest. Therefore, it is limited in most cases to projects with paid assistants. School psychologists, however, have found it a useful classroom observation tool for measuring ongoing behaviors such as the attending behavior of students referred to them by teachers.

In interval recording, each observation session is divided into equal periods. The observer then records the occurrence or nonoccurrence of behavior during these intervals. In the following illustration, the observer has recorded whether a child attended appropriately to an assigned task during 10-second intervals of a 2-minute observation period.

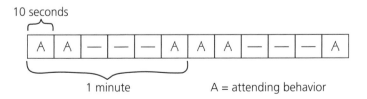

The observer wrote "A" during six intervals and "—" in the other six. This indicated the student attended during 6 (50%) of the 12 10-second intervals.

Whole or Partial Interval Recording

If the observer is using a *whole interval* recording procedure, the behavior must persist throughout the entire interval in order to be scored for that interval. If the observer is using a *partial interval* recording procedure, the behavior is scored for an interval if it occurs at all during the interval.

The whole interval recording procedure tends to underestimate the amount of behavior because intervals may not be scored for the behavior even though it occurred throughout most, but not all, of the interval. Therefore, behaviors we would like to have persist for long periods without interruption (such as work behavior) are usually measured using this procedure. The idea is that it is better to underestimate than to overestimate behavior we wish to increase in frequency. We must never use this procedure to measure brief behaviors (such as praise) that we want to increase in frequency because these behaviors may never last long enough to be scored.

The partial interval recording procedure tends to overestimate the amount of behavior because entire intervals will be scored for the behavior even if the behavior persists for only a brief part of the intervals. Therefore, behaviors we would like to weaken (such as disruptive behavior and hitting) are usually measured using this approach. It is better to overestimate behavior we wish to decrease in frequency than to underestimate it. We also use partial interval recording to measure brief behaviors that we wish to increase.

One weakness of interval recording is that it does not provide information on the actual number of times a behavior occurs or how long it occurs. It is better to use frequency or duration recording if it is important to know the frequency of a behavior or to know how long a behavior lasts.

Exercise

When should you use whole interval recording? _____

_____

When should you use partial interval recording? _____

_____

(continues)

The choice of the interval duration depends upon how often the behavior occurs. If it occurs very infrequently and you wish to decrease the behavior's frequency, then a long interval such as a minute will be adequate. However, if the behavior occurs quite often or you wish it to occur more often it would be best to use a brief interval duration such as 10 or 15 seconds.

When using interval recording, what determines the length of the interval?

_____

An example of an interval recording sheet follows this paragraph. You will notice that the interval length selected on this sheet is short (10 seconds). Suppose the behavior being observed (disruptive behavior) occurs frequently (as much as two or three times a minute). When studying disruptive behavior that occurs for brief periods, a partial interval recording procedure would be employed. The observer using this sheet begins observing by starting a stopwatch. If the behavior occurs at all during the first 10-second interval that box is checked. If not, the box is left blank or marked with a dot so that the observer can keep his or her place. The observer continues to observe. If the behavior occurs between seconds 10 and 20 of the first minute, the second box for the first minute is checked. This procedure is continued until the first minute is over, and then the observer begins scoring the second minute. Observers are able to record a behavior for several 10-minute observation periods using such a sheet. Because this method does not provide time for the observer to record behavior following each interval, it is difficult to use.

	0–10"	10"–20"	20"–30"	30"–40"	40"–50"	50"–60"	
Start							Min 1
							Min 2
							Min 3
							Min 4
							Min 5
							Min 6
							Min 7
							Min 8
							Min 9
							Min 10

One way to simplify the task is to alternate 10-second observing intervals with 5-second recording intervals when recording behaviors. Observers watch the first 10 seconds (0–10 seconds) of a minute and then record during the next 5 seconds (10–15 seconds). Then they observe for the next 10 seconds (15–25 seconds), and so on. Observers then do not miss behaviors while recording previous behaviors. Because looking at a stopwatch or timer can distract the observer from the task, it is often useful to prepare an audiotape to cue the observer to record behavior. The person making the recording would say "observe 1," meaning observer interval 1, at the start of the tape, and then say "record 1," meaning record what you saw during interval 1, 10 seconds later. After allowing 5 more seconds to elapse to allow the observer time to mark what he or she saw on the sheet, the person would say "observe 2." This procedure would be continued until the tape is finished. The observer can then listen to the tape through one earphone and use it to cue observation and recording times.

Exercise

Suggest two behaviors that could be observed using the whole interval recording procedure.

1. _____

2. _____

Suggest four behaviors that could be observed using the partial interval recording procedure.

1. _____

2. _____

3. _____

4. _____

Circle "event" or "duration" in the following sentences:

Most times it is better to use event / duration recording instead of partial interval recording.

Most times it is better to use event / duration recording instead of whole interval recording.

Interobserver Agreement

This is usually calculated by dividing agreements by agreements plus disagreements when using interval recording systems. One way is to count all cases where both observers agree that the behavior occurred (both observers marked the interval with a check or, if they are recording multiple behaviors, the same letter code), and all cases where both observers agree that the behavior did not occur (neither observer checked the box) as agreement. Disagreements are cases in which one observer scored the interval for the behavior and the other did not.

In Example 1 on the next page, two observers recorded disruptive classroom behavior independently. (They could not see each other's sheets while scoring the behaviors.) They began together with a prearranged signal, after first checking to make certain their stopwatches were in accord.

If we examine the sheets, we can see that both observers agreed that the behavior occurred during the first 10 seconds of the first minute and that it did not occur during the second 10 seconds of the first minute. They also agreed during the third interval (between 20–30 seconds) and the fifth interval (between 40–50 seconds). They disagreed during the fourth and sixth intervals. Thus, they agreed four times and disagreed twice during the first minute. These numbers have been written on the right of the sheet next to the 1-minute mark. They also agreed five times during the second minute and disagreed once during the fourth interval of this minute.

To calculate overall interobserver agreement, first score the remaining intervals for the number of agreements and disagreements, writing the numbers on the right. Then, total the two columns to get the total number of agreements and disagreements. Next, use the following formula:

$$\text{Percent interobserver agreement} = \frac{\text{number of agreements}}{\text{number of agreements} + \text{number of disagreements}} \times 100$$

You should have 86.6%.

Most researchers agree that average interobserver agreement should be at least 85% and that no single score should be below 70%. Furthermore, interobserver agreement should be high during both baseline and experimental or treatment conditions. These criteria are meant to be a guide. If the magnitude of the change produced is very large, lower levels of interobserver agreement may be acceptable. Conversely, if the change produced is very small, higher levels of interobserver agreement may be needed.

Researchers sometimes need to provide more information than is given by the overall measure of interobserver agreement. In these cases, two other

OBSERVER 1

0–10	10–20	20–30	30–40	40–50	50–60	MIN
✓	✓	✓	✓			1
✓	✓	✓				2
	✓			✓		3
	✓			✓		4
				✓	✓	5
✓		✓				6
						7
					✓	8
	✓					9
		✓	✓		✓	10

OBSERVER 2

MIN	0–10	10–20	20–30	30–40	40–50	50–60
1	✓		✓			✓
2	✓	✓	✓	✓		
3		✓	✓			
4		✓			✓	
5			✓			
6				✓		✓
7						
8	✓	✓				
9						
10	✓		✓	✓		✓

TOTAL

Percent interobserver agreement =

MIN	Number of Agreements	Number of Disagreements
1	4	2
2	5	1
3		
4		
5		
6		
7		
8		
9		
10		

Example 1.

types of interobserver agreement are separately calculated and presented. These are interobserver agreements on the occurrence and on the nonoccurrence of the behavior. To calculate interobserver agreement on the occurrence of a behavior, divide the number of times both observers agree that the behavior occurred by that number plus the number of times they disagreed. Interobserver agreement on nonoccurrence is calculated by dividing the number of times both observers agreed that the behavior did not occur by that number plus the number of times they disagreed.

In Example 2 on the next page, overall occurrence and nonoccurrence interobserver agreement has been calculated. This example shows that the occurrence and nonoccurrence forms of interobserver agreement are more exacting than the overall method of calculating interobserver agreement.

It is necessary to provide separate measures of interobserver agreement on occurrence and nonoccurrence of a behavior when you are looking at behavior that occurs almost all of the time or rarely.

A note of caution: When interobserver agreement is separately calculated for the occurrence and nonoccurrence of a behavior, it is possible that interobserver agreement on occurrence can be low if the behavior occurs very infrequently. Interobserver agreement on nonoccurrence can be low if the behavior occurs nearly all the time. Therefore, mean percentages of 75% or over are often considered adequate when this technique is employed.

In the observer record sheet on page 37, calculate overall occurrence and nonoccurrence interobserver agreement.

Momentary Time Sampling

This technique is similar to interval recording except that it does not require continuous observation. It is more convenient to use in most cases than duration or interval recording. However, it is not a good method to use to score infrequent short duration events because it is not likely you would observe such behaviors very often.

In time sampling the observer records ongoing behaviors only at the end of time intervals. Time sampling may be used by a parent who wants to estimate the percentage of time a child wears a hearing aid during the day, by a teacher who wishes to record a student's study behavior during a given period, or by an office manager who wants to record work behavior of a clerk. In the record of Bobby's Thumbsucking that follows, a parent wanted to know the percentage of time his child sucked his thumb at bedtime. The child was observed at prearranged intervals. These can be after fixed periods of time have elapsed, such as every 10 minutes. In the example, a 100-minute

OBSERVER 1						OBSERVER 2					Agree beh. occ.	Agree beh. didn't occ.	Overall agree	Overall disagree
0–15	15–30	30–45	45–60	MIN		0–15	15–30	30–45	45–60	MIN				
✓	✓		✓	1		✓	✓			1	2	1	3	1
✓		✓		2		✓				2	1	2	3	1
✓		✓		3		✓		✓		3	2	2	4	0
				4		✓		✓		4	1	3	4	0
✓		✓		5		✓				5	1	3	4	0
				6					✓	6	0	2	2	2
				TOTAL							7	13	20	4

Interobserver agreement:

$$\text{Overall} = \frac{\text{Overall agreement}}{\text{Overall agreements + disagreements}} = \frac{20}{20+4} = \frac{20}{24} = 83\%$$

$$\text{Occurrence} = \frac{\text{Agreements on occurrence}}{\text{Agreement on occurrence + disagreements}} = \frac{7}{7+4} = \frac{7}{11} = 64\%$$

$$\text{Nonoccurrence} = \frac{\text{Agreements on nonoccurrence}}{\text{Agreements on nonoccurrence + disagreements}} = \frac{13}{13+4} = \frac{13}{17} = 76\%$$

Example 2.

Exercise

Complete the calculations.

OBSERVER 1

0–10	10–20	20–30	30–40	40–50	50–60	MIN
✓	✓		✓		✓	1
	✓	✓	✓	✓		2
	✓		✓	✓		3
					✓	4
						5
		✓				6
	✓				✓	7
✓	✓		✓	✓		8
	✓		✓	✓		9
		✓		✓	✓	10
				✓		11
		✓				12
						13
✓	✓	✓			✓	14
		✓				15

OBSERVER 2

MIN	0–10	10–20	20–30	30–40	40–50	50–60
1		✓				✓
2		✓				✓
3		✓				
4		✓	✓			✓
5					✓	
6	✓			✓		
7		✓				
8			✓	✓	✓	
9	✓	✓		✓	✓	
10					✓	
11			✓			
12						
13			✓			
14	✓	✓				
15						

TOTAL

MIN	Number of Agreements on Occurrence	Number of Agreements on Nonoccurrence	Total Agreements	Total Disagreements
1	2	2	4	2
2	2	1	3	3
3				
4				
5				
6				
7				
8				
9				
10				
11				
12				
13				
14				
15				

Overall Interobserver Agreement = _____ = _____ %

Occurrence Interobserver Agreement = _____ = _____ %

Nonoccurrence Interobserver Agreement = _____ = _____ %

observation period was divided into ten, 10-minute intervals. At the end of each 10-minute period, the parent looked at Bobby and recorded whether the behavior was occurring at that instant. Because Bobby was put to bed each night at 9:00, the first observation was at 9:10, the second at 9:20, and so on. The last observation was at 10:40, just before the parents retired. If the child had his thumb in his mouth when the parent checked during any of the sample times, that time was scored with a check. It is important to determine if the person is engaging in the behavior at the exact time of the check. Do not score what the person was doing a minute before or after the sample time. In this example, the parent noted that Bobby's thumb was in his mouth at exactly 9:10, 9:20, 9:30 and 9:50, but not at 9:40.

Bobby's Thumbsucking

Time	9:10	9:20	9:30	9:40	9:50
Behavior	✓	✓	✓		✓
Time	10:00	10:10	10:20	10:30	10:40
Behavior					

Researchers frequently report time sample data as percentages. For example, Bobby was observed sucking his thumb during 4 of the 10 sampling times. Therefore, the percentage of sampled intervals in which Bobby sucked his thumb at bedtime on this night was 4/10 = 40%. The more often the behavior is sampled, the more closely the percentage of intervals in which the behavior occurs approximates the percentage of time that the behavior occurs.

Observers use time sampling to record many ongoing behaviors such as attending, glasses-wearing, typing, nail-biting, and so on. One parent recorded the percentage of time samples a boy was wearing an orthodontic device by sampling the behavior six times per day (Hall, Axelrod, et al., 1971).

Although time samples are frequently made at equal intervals, it is sometimes more practical to sample at irregular intervals. Some observers have used a kitchen timer set to ring at random times as a signal to remind them when to sample a behavior. This method eliminates the problem of remembering to sample the behavior at the end of a given interval. It also prevents the person being observed from learning in advance when sampling will occur. Irregular intervals can also be scheduled by recording a bell or tone on a tape and playing it back. If you record more intervals than you require, you can begin the tape at a different point each session.

The length of the intervals between observations is determined in part by the frequency of the behavior. If the behavior is of relatively short duration, frequent samples will have to be made. The time sample technique is generally used to record behaviors that are ongoing or that you would like to be ongoing. If this is not the case, it is more appropriate to use a frequency count or some other recording procedure.

Time sampling and frequency counting are the most useful techniques for measuring ongoing behavior. Unlike duration and interval recording, these techniques do not require the observer's continuous attention. (When possible, most observers make 5 or 10 samples per observation session. This makes it easier to compute percentages.)

Exercise

List four behaviors that could be recorded using a time sampling procedure.

1. _____

2. _____

3. _____

4. _____

Interobserver Agreement

This is calculated the same way as for interval recording. It is often sufficient to calculate overall interobserver agreement. On some occasions (usually when the behavior occurs most of the time or hardly ever), you may want to independently calculate interobserver agreement on the occurrence and nonoccurrence of a behavior.

The exercise on the next page reviews the calculation of these measures. Complete the calculations.

Placheck

There are many variations of time sampling. For example, Risley (1971) used a planned activity check (placheck) to sample the behavior of groups of

Exercise

Complete the calculations.

OBSERVER 1

Time	9:00	9:30	10:00	10:30
Behav.			✓	
Time	11:00	11:30	12:00	12:30
Behav.		✓	✓	
Time	1:00	1:30	2:00	2:30
Behav.		✓		✓
Time	3:00	3:30	4:00	4:30
Behav.			✓	✓

OBSERVER 2

Time	9:00	9:30	10:00	10:30
Behav.	✓		✓	✓
Time	11:00	11:30	12:00	12:30
Behav.			✓	
Time	1:00	1:30	2:00	2:30
Behav.		✓	✓	
Time	3:00	3:30	4:00	4:30
Behav.		✓	✓	

Agree on occ.	Agree on nonocc.	Total agree	Total disagree
2	1	3	1
1	2		

TOTAL

Overall interobserver agreement = _____ = _____%

Occurrence interobserver agreement = _____ = _____%

Nonoccurrence interobserver agreement = _____ = _____%

preschool children. At specified times observers counted how many children were engaged in each of several behaviors. By dividing these numbers by the total number of children present, it was easy to calculate the percentage of children engaged in each activity.

The following is a sample recording sheet. In this case there were 20 children present in the preschool.

	9:30	9:45	10:00	10:15	10:30	10:45	11:00
Painting	2	5	8	2	0	0	0
Playroom	5	5	2	8	10	10	10
Printing	3	3	0	0	0	0	0

The numbers in each box represent the number of children engaged in each activity at each of the sample times.

It is easy to see that the percentage of children engaging in these three activities changed over time, that more were in the playroom than were painting or printing, and that 10 of 20 (50%) were in the playroom during the last three checks. Adding the number of children painting, the number in the playroom, and the number printing does not have to total 20 because some of the children may not be engaged in any of the activities.

The placheck has been used to record the percentage of pupils in a preschool playing with toys and the percentage sleeping during nap time. In several studies it was also used to record the percentage of pupils seated at a certain table who were attending appropriately. The planned activity check technique can also be used to determine the percentage of workers attending to task in a business office or production line, or the percentage of athletes engaging in a variety of behaviors during practice.

Charlie Greenwood and his colleagues at the Juniper Gardens Children's Program have developed a recording system called the CISSAR to measure numerous aspects of teacher and student behavior using interval or momentary time sample techniques (Greenwood, Delquadri, & Hall, 1984). Observers use hand-held electronic recording devices to record classroom activity, task, structure, teacher position, teacher behavior, and a variety of student behaviors.

Exercise

List two behaviors of groups that might be sampled using a planned activity check procedure.

1. _____

2. _____

Interobserver agreement is calculated for planned activity checks in the same manner as for time sampling and interval recording. When the two counts are exactly the same they are scored as an agreement, and when they are different they are scored as a disagreement. The calculation of overall interobserver agreement is all that is required when planned activity checks are used to measure behavior.

▶ **Direct measurement of permanent product, automatic recording, behavior counts, checklists, duration or latency recording, and time sampling are much simpler and more flexible to use than ABC recording or interval recording.**

Exercise

Although you now should know many ways to record behavior, the difficult task is to know when to use each of these alternatives. For each of the following examples, select a method of recording and defend your choice.

Behavior	Method	Reason
1. Cleaning up	_____	_____
2. Teacher praise	_____	_____
3. Nap-taking (single child)	_____	_____
4. Written assignment completion	_____	_____

(continues)

5. Biting (2 or 3 times/day)   _____   _____

6. Long tantrums   _____   _____

7. Electricity consumption   _____   _____

8. Brushing teeth   _____   _____

9. Car use   _____   _____

10. Out-of-seat behavior   _____   _____

Table 1 lists the various recording methods, some examples of behaviors they are frequently used to measure, and the pros and cons associated with each.

It is often necessary to choose among several possible ways of recording a behavior. For example, someone interested in the amount of smoking in a public place could use behavior counts, time sampling, or permanent products (the number of cigarette butts in ashtrays or on the floor each day). The method selected depends upon the exact information needed and the resources available. For example, counting or weighing cigarette butts might be less labor-intensive but would not provide information on individual behavior such as how many cigarettes each person smoked.

Review Quiz 2

1. Define ABC recording.

_____

_____

2. What is the primary advantage of this technique?

_____

_____

(continues)

Table 1
Pros and Cons of Various Recording Methods

Method of Recording	Example of Behavior	Pros	Cons
Automatic Recording	A person's weight (scale). Mileage driven (odometer reading). Energy consumed (watt-hour meter). Tardiness at work (time clock). Aspects of academic or work performance (computers).	Precise. Highly objective. Quantitative. Easy to monitor. Can be used to obtain information on how often and how long a behavior occurs.	Can be expensive unless equipment is available. Lacks flexibility.
Permanent Product	Words correct on spelling test. The number of words keyboarded correctly per minute. Number of school windows broken per week. Number of pieces of litter on the ground in sample areas. Number of toys left on the floor.	Reasonably precise and objective. Not very expensive. Can usually be collected by staff without extra personnel.	Its use is restricted to behaviors that leave an enduring record.
ABC Recording	Useful whenever the situations associated with the behavior and the reinforcers maintaining the behavior have not been identified.	Can help identify situations that are associated with behaviors and reinforcers maintaining behaviors.	Not as accurate because the observer is looking at many potential situations and reinforcers at once.

(continues)

Table 1 (*Continued*)

Method of Recording	Example of Behavior	Pros	Cons
Behavior Counts	How often a student participates in classroom discussion. The number of times an employee leaves his or her work station. The number of times a student hits his or her peers. Days absent from school (behaviors with clear beginnings and ends).	Is easy for staff to use if the behavior is difficult to miss, such as tantrums. It does not require the observer's undivided attention. One of the most useful measurement techniques.	Not as convenient to use when the behavior does not attract the observer's attention.
Checklists	Number of recommended tasks included in a report. Number of safety related behaviors completed. Number of motorists yielding to pedestrians. Number of items completed on a clean room checklist.	A good way to record a number of critical steps or important tasks completed.	Does not yield data or information on the rate or duration of a behavior.
Duration Recording	How long employees spend on coffee breaks. How long a child spends crying when put to bed. How long a child spends reading each day.	Provides useful information when how long a behavior persists is the primary concern.	Requires the observer's undivided attention unless the beginning and end of the behavior is obvious (e.g., when someone enters or leaves a library or classroom).

(*continues*)

Table 1 (*Continued*)

Method of Recording	Example of Behavior	Pros	Cons
Latency Recording	How quickly a child follows instructions. How long it takes students to put away their materials. How long it takes an athlete to run a mile.	Is most important measure when the primary concern is how promptly or quickly a behavior occurs.	Same as above.
Whole Interval Recording	The percent of intervals a student spends studying. The percent of intervals employees spend working.	Most useful for behaviors you would like to persist.	Requires the observer's constant individual attention. Underestimates the amount of behavior.
Partial Interval Recording	The percent of intervals a child spends whining. The percent of intervals a child spends throwing a tantrum.	Most useful for behaviors that are only brief in duration (i.e., praise) or behaviors you would like to occur less often.	Requires the observer's undivided attention. Overestimates the amount of behavior.
Time Sampling	The percent of time a child plays with other children. The percent of time members of a swim team spend engaged in practice exercises.	Does not consume much of the observer's time (one of the most useful measurement techniques).	Time sampling is not useful when the behavior occurs infrequently, unless you wish to increase the behavior frequency.

3. Define behavior counts.

_____

_____

4. What is a major advantage of counting behavior?

_____

_____

5. Name four behaviors that should normally be measured by counting behavior.

a. _____

b. _____

c. _____

d. _____

6. Describe two ways of counting behavior.

a. _____

b. _____

7. In the example below, two observers marked down the time whenever Johnny threw a tantrum. Calculate the interobserver agreement.

Observer 1	Observer 2
9:50	9:50
1:33	1:33
2:15	2:15
3:00	2:25
3:30	3:00
4:20	3:30
	4:20

Interobserver agreement _____

(continues)

8. In the following example, two observers marked a tally every time Billy asked a question in class. Calculate the interobserver agreement.

Observer 1   ⅢⅢ ⅢⅢ ////

Observer 2   ⅢⅢ ⅢⅢ ⅢⅢ

Interobserver agreement _____

9. What is duration recording?

_____

_____

10. How is interobserver agreement reported when duration recording is used?

_____

_____

11. Define whole interval recording.

_____

_____

12. When should this method be used?

_____

_____

13. Define partial interval recording.

_____

_____

(continues)

14. When should this method be used?

    a. _____

    b. _____

15. Define time sampling.

    _____

    _____

16. When should this method be used?

    a. _____

    b. _____

17. In the following example, two observers recorded the percentage of time a receptionist spent working using time sampling. Calculate the overall percentage of interobserver agreement for this example.

Observer 1				Observer 2			
9:00	9:30	10:00	10:30	9:00	9:30	10:00	10:30
	✓	✓			✓	✓	
11:00	11:30	12:00	1:30	11:00	11:30	12:00	1:30
✓		✓		✓			
2:00	2:30			2:00	2:30		
				✓			

    Interobserver agreement _____

18. What criterion do behaviors have to meet to be scored with checklists?

    _____

    _____

Recording Etiquette

When using observational recording procedures in formal settings, it is important to follow some basic rules:

1. It is a good idea to have the teacher or supervisor introduce you with a statement about your interest in doing research.

2. Your entrance and departure should coincide with a natural break in routine such as snack time, lunch, or a change in activity. This creates the least amount of disruption of ongoing activity.

3. When two or more observers are present they should talk with each other as little as possible before and after observing and not at all during observation periods. Talking can cause sensitive persons (perhaps even a teacher) to conclude you are talking about them.

4. Do not talk to the individuals you are observing. If they talk to you, mention that you are busy and cannot talk while you are working, and then ignore further questions.

5. To prevent a specific child you are observing from becoming self-conscious, you should disguise your interest by varying the apparent object of your glances.

Graphing Behavior

Baseline

Once you have defined a behavior and selected a way of recording it, the next step is to measure the behavior over a period of time and graph the results. This establishes the level at which a behavior is occurring before attempting to modify it. The measurement of a behavior to establish its level in the absence of any systematic program is termed establishing a baseline. A *baseline* is a pre-experimental record of a behavior. The most effective way to represent a baseline is usually with a graph.

Exercise

A baseline is _____

Another term for baseline is *operant level*. Operant behavior operates on the environment or external world. It is selected by its consequences. Most human behavior such as talking, walking, hitting, shutting a door, studying, or making a sale are operant behaviors. How often such behaviors occur depends upon their consequences.

A conventional graph drawn on linear graph paper is often the easiest to use and to understand. Behavioral data displayed on conventional graph paper takes a standard format. The vertical axis (ordinate) is used to indicate the level or rate of a behavior, and the horizontal axis (abscissa) indicates the time dimension.

Figure 1 shows the number of problems a boy (John) worked correctly each day during his math period. The number of problems worked over a 6-day period was 2, 4, 6, 6, 10, and 10. This is an example of direct measurement of a lasting product. Note that the reliability of a second observer is indicated by a dot with an X through it on Days 2 and 5.

Figure 2 shows the number of times a girl (Jane) cried during seven 40-minute observation sessions on the preschool playground. The number of cries per session was 9, 9, 8, 6, 4, 2, and 3. This is an example of behavior counting. Note that the reliability observer's records are indicated by an X on Sessions 2 and 6.

Figure 3 is a graph of the number of minutes a girl (Debbie) was late for breakfast each day. Her record for eight days was 6, 8, 7, 8, 6, 7, 8, and 7. This is an example of _____ recording.

Figure 4 presents a record of the number of coffee breaks a secretary (Sue) had on consecutive days as recorded by her boss: 8, 4, 9, 3, 7, 5, 9, 2, 8, 4, 7, 4, 8. This is an example of _____.

By graphing compiled observational data, the observer creates a visual representation of the baseline level of the behavior. Because the slope of the curve made by joining the data points in Figure 1 is rising, we know the number of problems John is getting correct is increasing.

Ascending, Descending, and Level Baselines

A baseline record that shows an increase in behavior, as in Figure 1, is called an *ascending* baseline. A descending slope, as seen in Figure 2, illustrates a *descending* baseline. Figure 3, showing Debbie's late behavior, is an example of a *level* baseline, a record of a behavior which is neither increasing nor decreasing in slope.

(text continues on page 56)

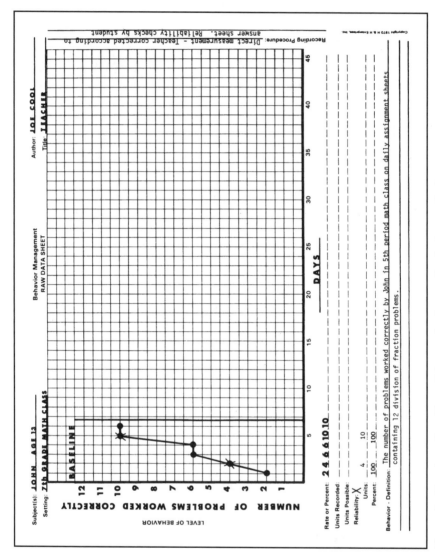

Figure 1. Number of problems John worked correctly during math class.

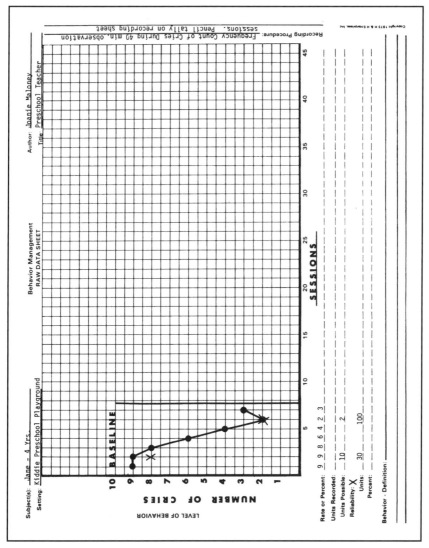

Figure 2. Number of times Jane cired during seven 40-minute observation sessions.

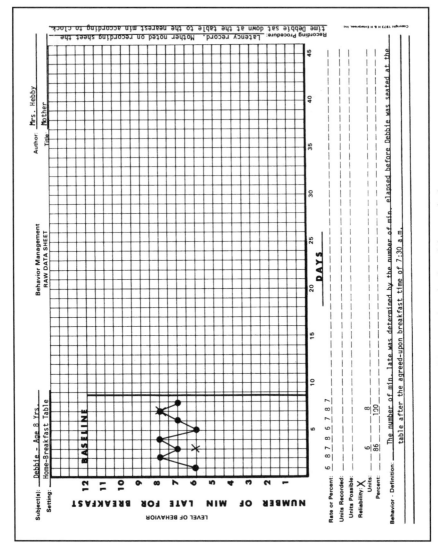

Figure 3. Number of minutes Debbie was late for breakfast each day.

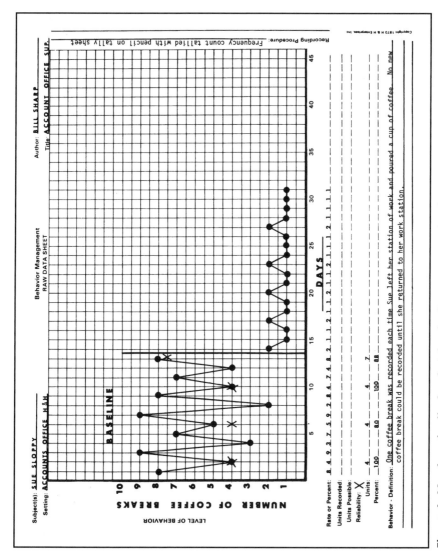

Figure 4. Number of coffee breaks taken by Sue on consecutive days.

Exercise

In the following examples, write whether each baseline is **ascending, descending,** or **level.**

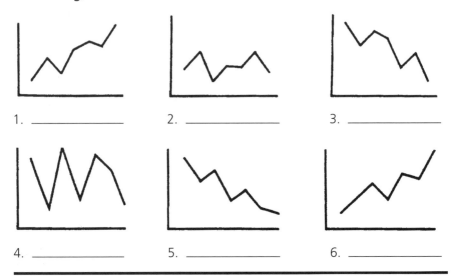

1. _____   2. _____   3. _____

4. _____   5. _____   6. _____

It takes as little as 5 or 6 days to determine whether a baseline is ascending, descending, or level. Sometimes it takes as many as 8 to 12 sessions. If you are uncertain whether the baseline is ascending, descending, or level it is sometimes best to extend the baseline for several more days until the type of baseline is clear. Without formally recording a baseline on a behavior, it is often difficult to be certain if an intervention technique has affected the behavior. Teachers, parents, and others often make imprecise statements about behavior such as "Maria continually disrupts the class," or "Bill is always out of his seat," or "John never types without making errors." Careful observation of the behaviors show that these statements exaggerate the problem. Conversely, individuals sometimes underestimate the extent of a problem. The main reason for obtaining a precise measurement of baseline rates is to be able to tell whether the modification procedures are affecting the behavior under study. Unless a record has been made, there is a danger that the behavior manager will assume that a change has been produced when no change has in fact occurred, or that a procedure is not effective when in fact it is producing a change in the behavior. When good graphic evidence exists, the behavior manager does not have to say, "I think he's improving," or "I don't think he's any better, so I guess we should try something else." Precise baseline data properly displayed on a graph leave no doubts about the effectiveness of a behavior management procedure.

Behavior sometimes begins to change during the baseline phase. The behavior manager should wait until the baseline levels off before beginning experimental procedures. Figure 1 shows that John's rate of working math problems accurately is increasing. Therefore, if new procedures are introduced to increase his math proficiency, and he works more problems correctly, the teacher would not be able to determine whether the modification procedures were responsible for the change.

For the same reason, if the principal introduced an experimental condition designed to reduce Jane's crying behavior (see Figure 2), and if her crying decreased, he could not say that his new condition caused the change because the crying was already decreasing.

In Debbie's case (see Figure 3), if her parents introduced an experimental condition which resulted in a sharp decrease in her being late for breakfast, the experimenter could say with some confidence that the experimental condition caused the decrease. Debbie's baseline record was quite level at around 7 minutes late for breakfast.

Experimental procedures can sometimes be initiated when a baseline is ascending, if the intent is to decrease the strength of the behavior, or, conversely, to begin experimental procedures when a baseline is descending, if the intent is to increase the strength of the behavior. This is done when it is desirable to reverse the trend of the behavior—for example, when a child is hitting his peers at an obviously increasing rate and it is important to decrease the hitting behavior as quickly as possible.

Variable Baselines

Another consideration is *variability*. Variability is the amount of day-to-day fluctuation in the behavior. Behaviors that vary little from day to day are called stable while data that show considerable change from day to day are called variable. It is generally easier to detect whether a treatment has produced a change when the baseline is stable than when it is highly variable.

For example, there is greater day-to-day variability in the number of Sue's coffee breaks (see Figure 4) than in the number of minutes that Debbie is late for breakfast (see Figure 3). Although Sue's record is as level as Debbie's, it shows much more erratic behavior. If you introduced a treatment that produced a reduction of 50% in the behavior of both girls, the change in Debbie's behavior would be more apparent than the change in Sue's.

Figure 5 illustrates this point. This example shows that you must produce a larger change in a behavior for it to be convincing when the behavior is highly variable.

The reason for this is the degree of overlap between baseline and treatment performance. The less the overlap, the more convincing the change. Generally, we are convinced that a change has actually occurred only when there is little or no overlap between performance during baseline and treatment conditions. Even when the degree of variability is fairly great, one may still be convinced that a change has occurred (provided the change produced is large enough). For example, in Figure 4 we see the effects of a treatment that produced a marked reduction in the number of Sue's coffee breaks.

It is necessary to produce larger changes to obtain convincing results when baseline data are highly variable. It is also necessary to observe the behavior for a longer time in order to determine if the baseline is level. The best way to tell if a baseline is level is to look at it. If it looks level, or if it fluc-

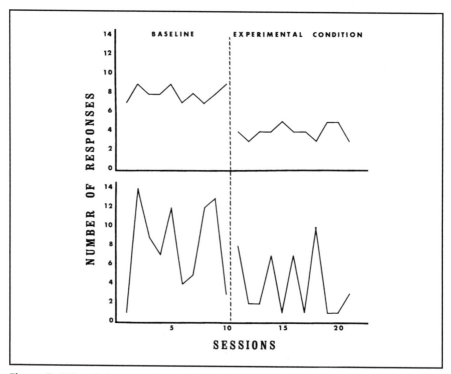

Figure 5. When behavior is highly variable, a larger change must be produced to be convincing.

tuates only within a given range, the observer is usually safe in assuming the baseline is stable. It is unwise to introduce a treatment when the data show a trend in the direction in which you wish to produce a change or when several data points suggest the possible beginning of such a trend. For example, the data presented in the following graph show that the behavior has increased during the last two days of measurement. A trained behavior analyst would not introduce a treatment designed to increase this behavior until the data have come back down or have stabilized at a new level.

 Exercise

In the following examples, decide whether a treatment should be introduced to increase the amount of behavior.

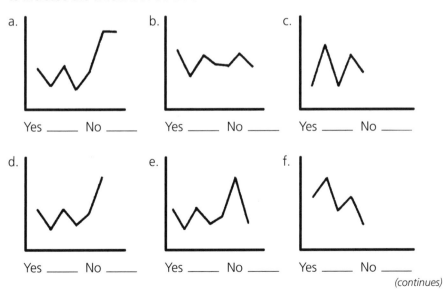

a.

Yes _____ No _____

b.

Yes _____ No _____

c.

Yes _____ No _____

d.

Yes _____ No _____

e.

Yes _____ No _____

f.

Yes _____ No _____

(continues)

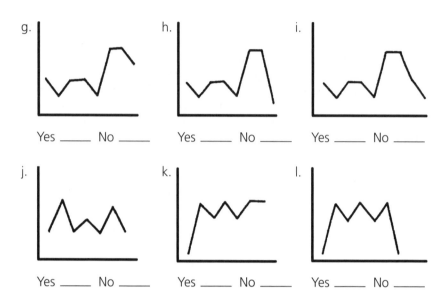

g.

Yes _____ No _____

h.

Yes _____ No _____

i.

Yes _____ No _____

j.

Yes _____ No _____

k.

Yes _____ No _____

l.

Yes _____ No _____

Answers: a. **No** b. **Yes** c. **Yes** d. **No** e. **Yes** f. **Yes** g. **No** h. **Yes** i. **Yes** j. **Yes** k. **Yes** l. **Yes**

Note: The pattern shown in "k" is typical of data sometimes obtained when the individuals observed have not had a chance to become used to the observer's presence before beginning the baseline. For this reason, some researchers do not count the first day of observation.

In cases in which the purpose of the treatment is to decrease a behavior, it is also important to postpone the introduction of a treatment when the data suggest the beginning of a downward trend.

Exercise

In the following examples, decide whether a treatment should be introduced to decrease the amount of behavior.

a.

Yes _____ No _____

b.

Yes _____ No _____

c.

Yes _____ No _____

d.

Yes _____ No _____

e.

Yes _____ No _____

f.

Yes _____ No _____

g.

Yes _____ No _____

h.

Yes _____ No _____

i. i.

Yes _____ No _____

j.

Yes _____ No _____

k.

Yes _____ No _____

l.

Yes _____ No _____

Answers: a. **Yes** b. **No** c. **Yes** d. **No** e. **No** f. **Yes**
g. **No** h. **Yes** i. **No** j. **Yes** k. **Yes** l. **Yes**

If you got most of these examples right, you are developing a good eye for behavior analysis.

Review Quiz 3

1. What are the five rules of recording etiquette?

    a. _____

    b. _____

    c. _____

    d. _____

    e. _____

2. What is a baseline? _____

    _____

3. Draw:

    a. an ascending baseline

    b. a descending baseline

    c. a level baseline

4. In the following examples, decide whether it would be wise to introduce a program to decrease the frequency of the behavior.

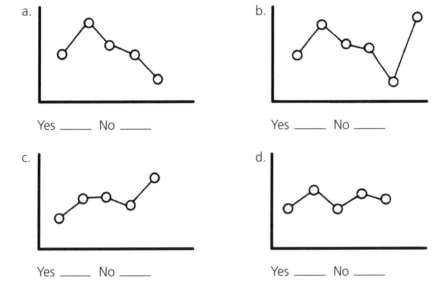

a.

Yes _____ No _____

b.

Yes _____ No _____

c.

Yes _____ No _____

d.

Yes _____ No _____

e.

Yes _____ No _____

f.

Yes _____ No _____

Measures of Central Tendency

It is usually possible to estimate the operant level of a behavior by looking at a graphed baseline. In preparing data for presentation, however, it is best to report the central tendency of the record in numerical terms. There are two basic ways commonly used to express central tendency, the mean and the median. The mean number of behavior occurrences is the arithmetic average, which is computed by adding the number of behavior occurrences per day and dividing that total by the number of days of observation. In the following example, Bill sold 6, 7, 5, 5, 4, 4, 8, 7, and 6 computers on different days. The mean number of computers sold is 5.77.

```
6
7
5              5.77      rounded to the nearest
5           9)52         tenth becomes 5.8
4             45
4             70
8             63
7             70
6
──
52
```

The median is the middle score. It is found by ranking the scores from lowest to highest, or from highest to lowest, and then finding the middle score. In the following example, Frank used curse words 6, 7, 5, 5, 4, 4, 8, 7, and 6 times on different days. The median number of curse words is 6 because there are 4 scores above it and 4 scores below it.

```
8
7
7
6
6     median score = 6
5
5
4
4
```

When the number of scores is even the median is the mean of the middle two scores. In the following example, the median of 6, 8, 4, 3, 9, 12, 4, 8 is 7.

```
3
4
4
6     6 and 8 are the middle two scores
8     the mean of 6 and 8 is (6 + 8) ÷ 2, or 7
8
9
12
```

The mean and the median are usually close to each other and in some cases are identical. Either or both can be used in measuring central tendency, and either or both can be displayed as horizontal lines on a graph.

The points on a conventional graph do not necessarily have to be joined, but it does make them easier to read. Bar graphs (histograms) are sometimes used rather than line graphs. They are as valid as line graphs and are more useful than other types of graphs when presenting some kinds of data. Make a histogram of Frank's curse-word behavior.

Review Quiz 4

Find the median and the mean of the following two series of numbers:

3, 4, 6, 7, 5, 5, 6

9, 8, 7, 6, 7, 8

1. Median = _____   Mean = _____

2. Median = _____   Mean = _____

Note: If the median falls between two scores, take the midpoint between them.

Applied Behavior Analysis Research Designs

Traditional educational research finds correlations between certain conditions or procedures and the behaviors of pupils. One favored method used in education is to compare two groups of pupils who differ on one dimension to see how they differ on another dimension. This research shows that knowledge of subject matter, being well liked, a firm tone of voice, a good sense of humor, and various other teacher characteristics are correlated with good classroom control. Unfortunately, such research does not demonstrate direct causal relationships, nor does it address individual behavior problems or prescribe specific teacher procedures for managing classroom behavior.

Another approach to research has been the control-group/experimental-group design. In this approach, two groups are equated as closely as possible. Performance is measured in both groups, then one group is exposed to experimental procedures and the other group is not. Again, performances are compared and any statistical difference in performance is attributed to experimental procedures. This design is limited because it can be used only for comparing groups. It is useless for studying individual behaviors. Further, the requirement that individuals be randomly assigned to conditions cannot always be met unless subjects are studied for only a brief time in an artificial setting. With this design, statistics are applied after the experiment is completed to determine the likelihood that the experiment would yield the same results if repeated. An alternative way of answering this question is to repeat the experiment and see if the same results are obtained. This more direct approach is called *replication*, and it is the oldest and most reliable method used in scientific inquiry.

In recent behavioral research, several basic designs have been developed to emphasize baseline logic and replication to assess the reliability of research findings. These designs can be applied to single subjects or to single groups. All these designs allow managers to scientifically verify whether their procedures are really responsible for changes in behavior.

Advantages of Replication Designs

Replication designs offer the following advantages over standard group designs:

• It is not necessary to randomly assign participants to a treatment and a control group with replication-based designs. Without random assignment, a group design is invalid. Moreover, you have to ensure that there are no other differences between the treatment and control groups besides the presence or absence of the treatment. For example, if you wished to compare two reading programs for first-grade students, you will not have a true experiment if you randomly assign children to two different classrooms because, in addition to having different programs, the two classrooms also have other things that are not common such as different teachers. Instead you would need to randomly assign many classrooms to the control and treatment condition so that the teacher variable is randomly assigned to the treatment and control groups. This would add to the time and effort needed to complete the experiment. Replication-based designs that involve repeated measures are an easier way to address this problem.

• You do not require a large number of participants to use replication-based designs. Many times you do not have access to a large enough sample of people to fulfill the needs of a group design. For example, a therapist may be working with only one or two children with autism, or a parent may need to change the behavior of only one child. Another advantage of working with a small number of individuals, classrooms, or workers is that it allows one to more closely supervise the experiment. This is particularly important when trying new treatments that require close supervision.

• You do not need an untreated control group with replication-based designs. Therefore, it is possible to offer a potentially helpful program to all those who could benefit from it rather than only the half in a treatment group.

• Replication-based research designs allow the person conducting the study to determine whether the treatment worked for each individual. Typically, group designs inform the person conducting the study only whether the treatment scores were significantly different from the control group scores. A replication design allows one to determine who responded favorably, who did not respond, and who responded negatively to the treatment. This puts the researcher or practitioner in a position to determine individual factors which are associated with positive outcomes.

• Replication-based designs allow the researcher to control sources of variability and make changes to the treatment if it does not work as expected. Such a problem-solving approach leads to more rapid development of effective treatments. This advantage of replication-based designs is probably one of their strongest points.

The AB Design

The AB design gets its name from its two phases. The first phase (A) is a pre-experimental or baseline phase before experimental manipulation. In the second phase (B), an experimental treatment is applied in an attempt to bring about change in the behavior.

In the following examples of AB designs, one treatment has increased a behavior and one has resulted in a decrease in responding.

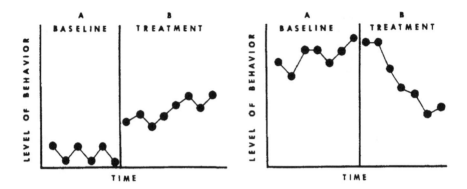

AB designs are the least convincing of applied behavior analysis designs. What power they have derives from baseline logic. That is, the baseline data indicate that if nothing were done about these behaviors they would probably remain at the baseline (A) levels. However, because the behaviors changed abruptly when the treatment phases (B) began, one can infer that the treatment caused the change.

But the AB design provides relatively weak evidence that the treatment condition brought about the observed change. Any of a number of coincidental factors could have brought about the change in behavior. In fact, there are instances in which researchers have recorded a level baseline and have been prepared to introduce an experimental treatment procedure only to have the behavior suddenly change in the desired direction just before they began implementing the treatment procedure. Therefore, most researchers prefer to use designs other than the AB design.

The Reversal Design

Reversal is one of the most fundamental designs in behavior analysis. It relies on both baseline logic and replication for its power. The following steps are used in employing a reversal design to investigate the effects of a given condition on a specific behavior:

1. **Baseline$_1$:** Scientifically define and record the operant level of the behavior prior to the institution of experimental conditions.

2. **Experimental Condition 1:** After you are convinced that the baseline data are sufficiently stable and that there is no compromising trend in the data, begin the experimental procedures while continuing to record the amount of behavior.

3. **Baseline₂:** Withdraw the experimental procedure. Return to the conditions that prevailed during Baseline 1 and continue to measure the behavior.

4. **Experimental Condition 2:** Reinstate the experimental procedures. Return to the conditions that prevailed during the first experimental condition.

The introduction of the reversal helps verify the assumption of the baseline logic. That is, if treatment had not been introduced the behavior would have remained at baseline levels. The second introduction of the experimental conditions (Step 4) allows one to replicate the effects produced during their first introduction (Step 2). Hence, the original effects of the experimental condition are replicated one time. Figure 6 shows how the reversal design was used to demonstrate the causal relationship between teacher attention and the disputing behavior of a 15-year-old boy (Hall, Fox, et al., 1971).

Note: Experimental phases may be divided by vertical lines. Data points between conditions are not joined. Data points during postchecks are not joined. Experimental conditions are labeled as descriptively as possible.

It is usually sufficient to replicate a finding only once by following a return to baseline conditions with a second introduction of the experimental conditions. However, if you have some overlap between the amount of behavior during baseline and experimental conditions, you may choose to perform one or more additional replications to see whether the effects observed were, in fact, caused by the experimental conditions. This is one

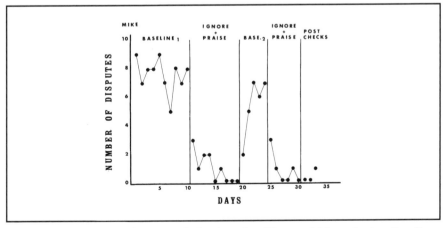

Figure 6. A record of disputing behavior of a 15-year-old boy during Baseline₁, Ignore and Praise, Baseline₂, Ignore and Praise, and Post Check conditions.

way of making equivocal results more clear. You may recall that another way involves more carefully controlling relevant variables.

In order to further replicate a finding, the researcher need only withdraw the experimental treatment a third time (this condition would be termed Baseline 3), and reintroduce the treatment again (this condition would be termed Experimental Condition 3). Once the effects are convincing, the final condition is termed a post check or follow-up. During this condition, the behavior is periodically measured to see if the changes produced are being maintained. This helps evaluate whether the treatment's effects are durable.

Evaluating Whether the Treatment Produced a Change

Analysis of results with replication designs that use repeated measures usually requires visual inspection of the data. In evaluating whether a change took place, the experienced researcher must consider the following:

1. How large is the change compared to the pretreatment level of the behavior? Typically, we are looking for robust effects that would make a difference in a person's life.

2. What is the degree of overlap between the baseline and treatment data paths? Typically, we would like to see little or no overlap between baseline and treatment results. Ideally, we would like to see the lowest point during the treatment condition greater than the highest point during the baseline when we are introducing a program to increase behavior, or the highest point during treatment lower than the lowest point during baseline when we are trying to decrease behavior.

3. No trend exists in the baseline that would predict the change produced by the treatment. Ideally, the baseline should be level or decreasing when we wish to increase a behavior, or level or increasing when we wish to decrease a behavior.

The examples presented in the top portion of Figure 7 illustrate how these criteria interact. These graphs show how it is easier to detect a small difference when there is little or no overlap between baseline and treatment data. The difference in the mean level of behavior is the same in both graphs, but the effect is more apparent in the right-hand graph because of the lower level of day-to-day variation (variability) in the data.

The pair of graphs in the lower portion of the figure shows how a large change can be apparent even if there is a high level of variability. Both graphs have similar levels of day-to-day variation (variability), but only the large treatment effect on the right is apparent.

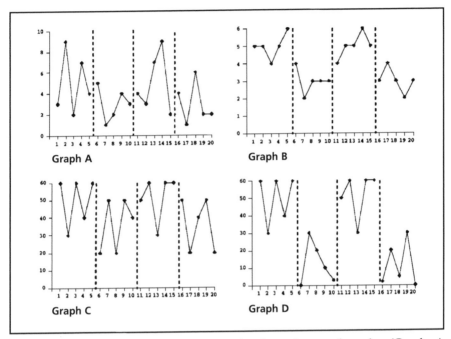

Figure 7. Examples of reversal designs with a large degree of overlap (Graphs A and C) and little overlap (Graphs B and D).

Statistics and Replication Logic Designs

Although there is no good reason why statistical analysis could not be applied to replication-based designs, it is not necessary because the data so far exceed the standard for significance that formal calculations are unnecessary. For example, taking the data from graph D, it is clear that all treatment data points lie below the baseline mean. Assuming (a) no trend, a reasonable assumption with this data, and (b) no treatment effect (the null hypothesis), one would expect that half the data points during the treatment would be below the baseline mean and half above it. Therefore, the probability of any point being below the baseline mean is 0.5. The probability of all 5 points being below is 0.5 raised to the 5th power. The probability of all points during the second baseline phase being above the treatment mean is again 0.5 raised to the 5th power.

The probability of all points during the second treatment phase being below all baseline points is again 0.5 to the 5th power. Since we predicted all the directions of change, the probability of all this happening by chance is 0.5

to the 18th power. This would be a probability of .0000038. It should be pointed out that this is a conservative estimate because this is the probability that all points are above or below the mean of baseline not above all points. Clearly many findings which would be rejected by someone in the field of behavior analysis would be accepted by someone who applied significance testing using the .05 confidence level. The reason behavior analysts do not look for less robust effects is that they distrust data with a lot of overlap. If a lot of overlap exists, it implies that there are many powerful variables responsible for the behavior swings on a day-to-day basis that are as powerful as the treatment being evaluated. These other variables may interact in unknown ways with the treatment effect and the treatment effect may be dependent on such variables to a certain degree. Because these factors have not been identified it is difficult to know their status in future applications. This weakens confidence in the effects.

Limitations of the Reversal Design

At least two factors limit the usefulness of the reversal design. Some changes in behavior are permanent. Also, there are times when you might prefer not to return to baseline conditions for ethical reasons.

Reversibility

Many times the changes we produce in behavior are maintained by other factors beyond our control. In these cases, a return to baseline conditions will not be associated with a return of the behavior to baseline levels. For example, a program designed to teach a child with a development delay to ride a bicycle may be needed to efficiently produce bicycle-riding behavior, but once the behavior is produced, the natural consequences of riding a bicycle are usually sufficient to maintain this behavior. We are often pleased when our programs produce effects that endure when they are removed. In many cases, however, the removal of the experimental conditions leads to a return to baseline levels of performance. In these cases, the reversal design is quite effective.

Is an experimental condition really useful if performance deteriorates each time the experimental condition is removed? The frequent value of such experimental conditions can be easily illustrated by a few examples. It has long been known that posting reasonable speed limits reduces vehicle speeds and accidents. It is also known that removal of these signs leads to an increase in speeding behavior. We can conclude that to maintain safer roads we must leave posted speed limits in effect all of the time. A similar argument can be made for the placement of stop signs at dangerous intersections, or for persons with insulin dependent diabetes taking insulin, or for persons who require glasses wearing them every time they drive. Sometimes an experimental treatment is a better way of doing things and should be maintained instead of the less effective techniques previously employed.

Another point to consider is that the effects of some experimental conditions prove irreversible once they have been in effect for a sufficient time. Researchers are well advised to carry out a reversal as soon as possible after an experimental procedure brings about a convincing behavior change. Waiting longer may require a longer reinstatement of baseline in order to observe a reversal effect, or it is possible that there will be no reversal at all. Removing the experimental treatment for a brief period at various times during follow-up can help to determine whether the effects of the experimental condition are beginning to become permanent.

Ethical considerations sometimes preclude the use of the reversal design. For example, it is unwise to use the reversal design when studying dangerous problems. In these cases it is far better to use one of the alternative designs.

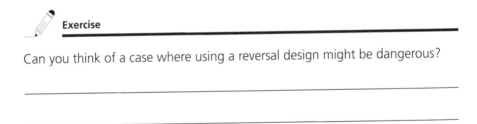

Exercise

Can you think of a case where using a reversal design might be dangerous?

_____

_____

The Multiple Baseline Design

There are several ways to use the multiple baseline design, but all follow the same basic pattern. The following steps are used in employing the multiple baseline design across individuals or groups of individuals:

1. **Baseline:** Concurrently record the behavior of two or more persons.

2. **Experimental Conditions:** (a) Begin experimental conditions with only one person until a change in behavior is observed; (b) begin the same experimental procedures with the second person; (c) successively begin experimental procedures with the third person, and so on.

The graph in Figure 8 shows how a multiple baseline design was used to demonstrate the causal relationship between improved grades in a high school French class and the teacher's offer to work with three pupils after school if they received D or F grades on daily French quizzes.

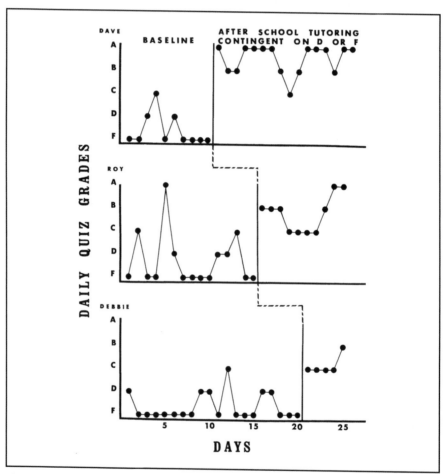

Figure 8. A record of daily French quiz grades of 3 high school students during Baseline and After School Tutoring Contingent on D or F grade conditions. *Note.* From "Teachers and parents as researchers using multiple-baseline design," by R. V. Hall, C. Cristler, S. Cranston, and B. Tucker, 1970, *Journal of Applied Behavior Analysis, 3,* pp. 247–255. Copyright 1970 by Journal of Applied Behavior Analysis. Reprinted with permission.

It is also possible to use a multiple baseline design across groups of individuals such as different classrooms, different shifts, or different teams. However, the basic elements of the design remain the same. First, baseline records are collected on several different groups. Next, the experimental procedure is introduced for one of the groups. When the performance of the first group shows a clear change, the procedure is introduced for the next group, and so on. The graph in Figure 9 shows how a multiple baseline design was used to evaluate a program designed to increase yielding by drivers to pedestrians.

Multiple baseline designs can also be used with different behaviors emitted by the same individual. In this design, baselines are recorded on two or more behaviors. Then, the experimental procedure is introduced for one behavior at a time. The graph in Figure 10 illustrates how a multiple baseline across behaviors can be used.

Multiple baseline designs can also be employed with the same individual emitting the same behavior in several situations (such as in the presence of two different teachers), in several settings (such as at home or in school), or at different times (such as in the morning and in the afternoon). Again, the experimental procedure is introduced to each situation, setting, or time of day successively. In the example in Figure 11, a multiple baseline across different times design has been combined with a reversal design.

Multiple baseline designs have the advantages of both baseline logic and replicability. The baselines indicate the level the behavior would probably maintain if no intervention were introduced, and the change brought about in the first behavior is replicated when the treatment is introduced for subsequent behaviors.

However, because multiple baseline designs do re-establish baseline level, trend effects have a marked influence upon whether the treatment is judged effective. This is illustrated in the examples in Figure 12. Although there is no overlap between the data in either example, only the data on the right is convincing because the baseline did not show any apparent trend. In the case of the data shown on the left, it is likely that this data path would have continued its upward trend even if the treatment had not been introduced.

To summarize, the multiple baseline design is a very flexible research design that does not require that a change produced by an experimental procedure be reversible. Multiple baseline designs can be introduced across individuals, groups, behaviors, situations, settings, and time of day. The only restriction that a multiple baseline design places on the experimenter is that the baselines be independent. If they are not, a change in one baseline will produce a change in the others, thereby making it difficult to demonstrate

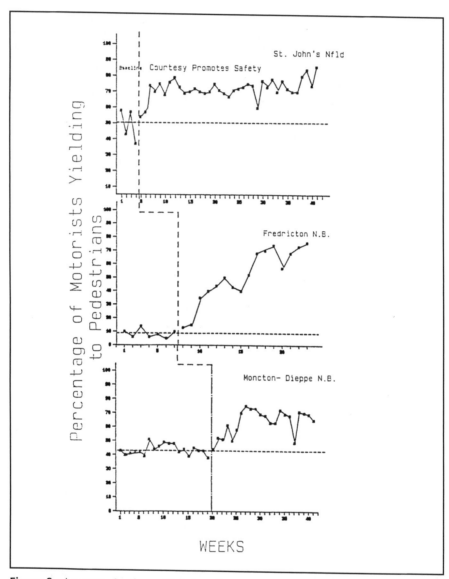

Figure 9. An example of a multiple baseline across groups. The graph shows the percentage of motorists yielding to pedestrians each week in three cities before and after treatment. *Note.* From "Increasing the percentage of drivers yielding to pedestrians in Canadian cities with a multifaceted safety program," by J. E. L. Malenfant and R. Van Houten, 1989, *Health Education Research Theory and Practice, 5,* 275–279. Copyright 1989 by Oxford University Press. Reprinted with permission.

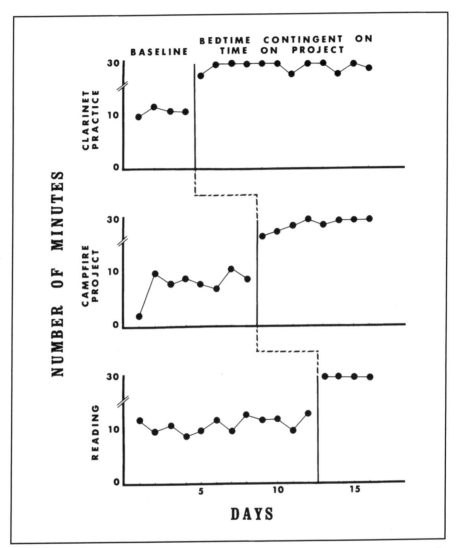

Figure 10. A record of time spent in clarinet practice, campfire honors project work, and reading for book reports by a 10-year-old girl. *Baseline*—before experimental procedures. *Early Bedtime Contingent on Less Than 30 Min. of Behavior*—1 min. earlier bedtime for each minute less than 30 engaged in an activity. *Note.* From "Teachers and parents as researchers using multiple-baseline design," by R. V. Hall, C. Cristler, S. Cranston, and B. Tucker, 1970, *Journal of Applied Behavior Analysis, 3,* pp. 247–255. Copyright 1970 by Journal of Applied Behavior Analysis. Reprinted with permission.

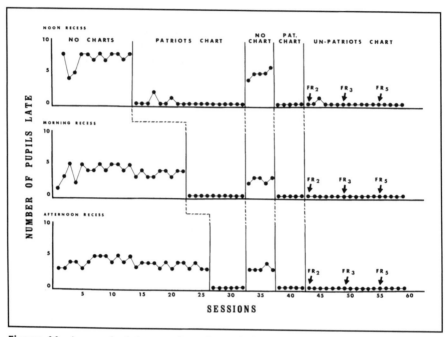

Figure 11. A record of the number of pupils late in returning to their fifth-grade classroom after noon, morning, and afternoon recess. *No Charts*—baseline, before experimental procedures. *Patriots' Chart*—posting of pupil names on Today's Patriots' chart contingent on entering class on time after recess. *No Chart*—posting of names discontinued. *Patriots' Chart*—return to Patriots' Chart conditions. *Un-Patriots' Chart*—posting of names on "Un-Patriots'" chart contingent on being late after recess every two days (FR 2), every three days (FR 3), and every five days (FR 5). *Note.* From "Teachers and parents as researchers using multiple-baseline design," by R. V. Hall, C. Cristler, S. Cranston, and B. Tucker, 1970, *Journal of Applied Behavior Analysis, 3,* pp. 247–255. Copyright 1970 by Journal of Applied Behavior Analysis. Reprinted with permission.

experimental control. In this regard, the multiple baseline design applied across individuals and groups most often meets the requirement of independent baselines.

The multiple baseline design applied across situations and behaviors most often meets the requirements of independent baselines when the situa-

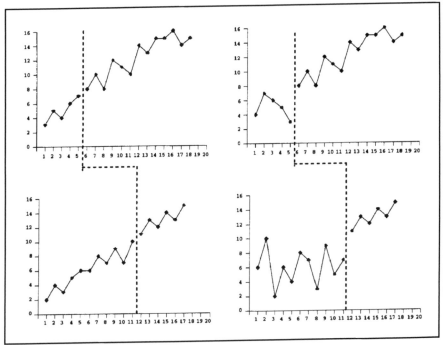

Figure 12. The graphs on the left show multiple baselines with ascending baselines while the graphs on the right show multiple baselines with stable baselines.

tions or behaviors are very different. Similar situations or behaviors are the most likely to generalize from treated to untreated situations or behaviors. For example, it is more likely that a change in behavior produced in one math skill (addition) will generalize to a similar math skill (subtraction) than to a totally different task (reading). However, it should be noted that if the treatment involves a behavior that is easily transferred, such as teaching students how to check their work, the treatment may affect both behaviors.

It is possible to combine elements of the reversal and multiple baseline designs. If you suspect that a treatment effect will not be reversible, you can first use a multiple baseline design to demonstrate the effectiveness of the experimental procedure, and then remove and reintroduce the treatment to verify whether the effects produced were, in fact, irreversible.

Exercise

List the various ways a multiple baseline design can be employed.

1. across _____

2. across _____

3. across _____

4. across _____ , _____ , or _____

Alternating Treatments Design

The alternating treatments design is a specialized design used to compare two or more different experimental procedures. The following steps are used to employ an alternating treatments design to compare the effects of two experimental conditions on a specific behavior.

1. **Baseline 1:** Determine the operant level of the behavior prior to the institution of experimental conditions. The length of the observation period should be from 45–90 minutes.

2. **Experimental Condition 1:** During this condition, one of the two experimental conditions is present during the first third of the observation period, baseline is in effect during the middle third of the observation period, and the second experimental condition is present during the final third of the period. The order in which the two treatments are presented each day should be randomly determined by the flip of a coin. The baseline need not be applied during the experimental condition in all cases.

The graph in Figure 13 shows how an alternating treatments design was used to compare the effects of verbal reprimands delivered alone to verbal reprimands delivered along with nonverbal disapproval consisting of a stare and holding the child by the shoulders. *Note:* The alternating treatments design has been combined with the reversal design in Figure 13.

Because both experimental conditions and the baseline condition are in effect for some of the time each day, uncontrolled factors that cause behavior

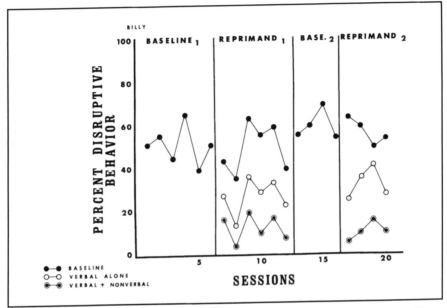

Figure 13. A record of disruptive behavior of an elementary student during Baseline₁; Baseline, verbal reprimands and verbal plus nonverbal reprimands₁; Baseline₂; and Baseline, verbal reprimands and verbal reprimands plus nonverbal reprimands₂. *Note.* From "An Analysis of Some Variables Influencing the Effectiveness of Reprimands," by R. Van Houten, P. A. Nau, S. E. Mackenzie-Keating, D. Sameoto, and B. Colavecchia, 1982, *Journal of Applied Behavior Analysis, 15,* pp. 65–83. Copyright 1982 by Journal of Applied Behavior Analysis. Reprinted with permission.

to fluctuate on a day-to-day basis affect each of the experimental conditions more or less equally. This is one reason why this design is so effective in detecting differences between two different experimental conditions. The continuation of a period when baseline conditions are in effect helps to assess whether the overall level of the behavior is changing.

The effectiveness of the alternating treatments design can be enhanced by pairing an instruction or another clear stimulus with each of the conditions. In Figure 14, the alternating treatments design was employed to compare whether a boy worked harder when he worked for himself alone or when he worked for himself plus the rest of the class. To make it clear to the boy under which condition he was working, instructions were presented at the beginning of each condition.

Figure 15 shows the use of an alternating treatments design that compares two signals to alert motorists that a pedestrian is crossing the street in

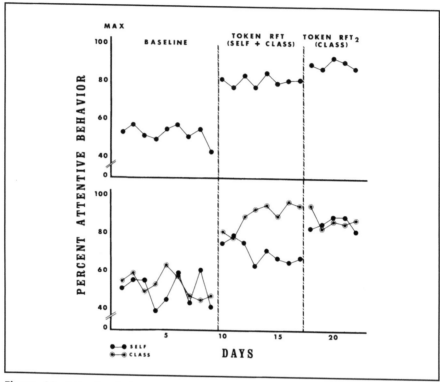

Figure 14. Attentive behavior of boy across experimental conditions. *Baseline*—no experimental intervention. *Token reinforcement (token rft)*—implementation of the token program where tokens earned could purchase events for himself (self) or the entire class (class). *Second phase of token reinforcement (token rft₂)*—implementation of the class exchange intervention across both time periods. The upper panel presents the overall data collapsed across time periods and interventions. The lower panel presents the data according to the time periods across which the interventions were balanced, although the interventions were presented only in the last two phases. *Note.* From "Simultaneous Treatment Design," by A. E. Kazdin and S. Geesey, 1977, *Behavior Therapy, 8,* pp. 682–693. Copyright 1977 by Academic Press. Reprinted with permission.

a crosswalk located in the middle of the block. The first signal was a flashing yellow beacon. The second signal was a picture of a pedestrian showing the direction he or she is traveling and eyes that look back and forth to prompt the motorist to look for the pedestrian. Both signals were put up at the same intersection. Each day the observers flipped a coin to determine whether to

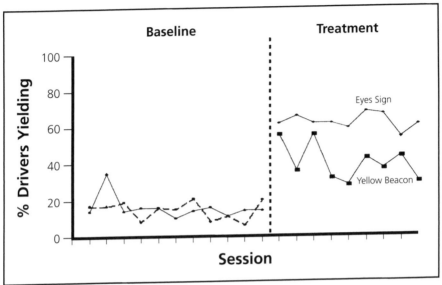

Figure 15. An example of an alternating treatments design that compares the effectiveness of two different traffic signals.

start with the beacon or the signal with the pedestrian symbol and eyes looking back and forth. Whichever signal won the toss was activated by a switch in the signal control cabinet. Once data were collected for the first signal, the switch was flipped to activate the other signal. The data in Figure 15 show that the sign with the pedestrian signal and moving eyes was much more effective than the flashing beacon.

One drawback of using the alternating treatments design is that it may not discriminate among treatments during the acquisition phase of an irreversible behavior. That is, one treatment may bring about improvement in behavior while a second treatment, though ineffective, may show improvement whereas, in reality, the behavior was merely being maintained at the new level brought about by the first treatment. Hence, its use is limited to comparing the effects of several reversible conditions or treatments.

Designs that Vary the Criterion or Intensity of a Treatment

Some designs involve varying the criterion for the treatment or the intensity of the treatment over time. One advantage of this type of design is that it is not necessary to perform a reversal or to employ multiple baselines.

Changing Criterion Design

The changing criterion design (Hall, 1971; Hall & Fox, 1977) has elements of both baseline logic and replication, and demonstrates control during shaping. In the changing criterion design, a baseline is generated on a single target behavior. Baseline is followed by a series of behavior change phases. Each phase is associated with a stepwise change in the criterion for reinforcement or punishment of the target behavior. When the criterion performance has been reached in the first behavior change phase, a new criterion level is established for the second phase. When the criterion performance has been met in the second phase, a new criterion level of performance is required in the next phase and through all subsequent phases until the desired target level of performance is reached. In this manner, each phase of the design provides a baseline for the following phase which, in turn, provides a baseline for the next phase.

Usually a stability criterion is used. For example, the criterion level for one phase may be maintained for three consecutive observation sessions before the criterion is changed to a new level. This indicates that responding is stable around the criterion and that advancing to the next criterion level might be indicated.

The more neatly the behavior conforms to the criteria changes, the more convincing the experimental control. It is possible to demonstrate further control by leaving the criterion at an established level for a longer time than is indicated by the stability criterion. For example, if the behavior must conform to a criterion for three days, it can remain at that level for five days before moving to the next criterion level. It is also possible to return to a former criterion level. If the behavior conforms to this criterion in what amounts to a partial reversal, a high degree of experimental control is indicated.

In the example in Figure 16, both of these strategies were employed. The 9-minute criterion was held in effect for 5 days and the criterion of performance was decreased from 12 to 9. The graph shows how a changing criterion design made the opportunity to spend time on the computer contingent on performance in working math problems by a student who did not usually complete his work. The boy's performance in solving math problems changed in conformity with the changing criterion levels until the desired terminal performance level of 12 problems correct was consistently achieved.

Intensified Treatment Design

This design can be used when it is not possible to employ a reversal design and where the presence of only one baseline precludes the use of the multiple

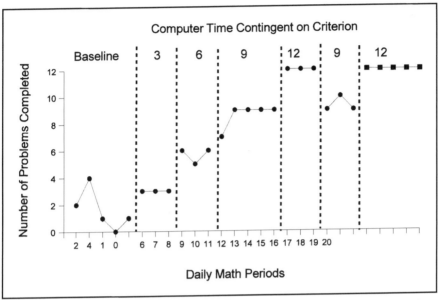

Figure 16. A record of the number of math problems correctly solved by a student during baseline and during a condition in which he could earn the opportunity to spend time on the computer contingent on changing levels of performance.

baseline design. The following steps investigate the effects of a given experimental condition on a behavior.

1. **Baseline 1:** Record the operant level of the behavior.

2. **Experimental Condition, First Intensity:** After you are convinced that the baseline data are sufficiently stable, introduce the experimental procedures at a weak intensity.

3. **Experimental Condition, Second Intensity:** After you are convinced that performance has stabilized under the first intensity of the experimental conditions (you must be perfectly sure that there is no improving trend), you introduce the experimental treatment at an even higher intensity.

Figure 17 shows how an intensified treatment design can assess the effects of teacher praise on student task performance. It is also possible to enhance the effectiveness of the procedure by increasing the amount of reinforcement.

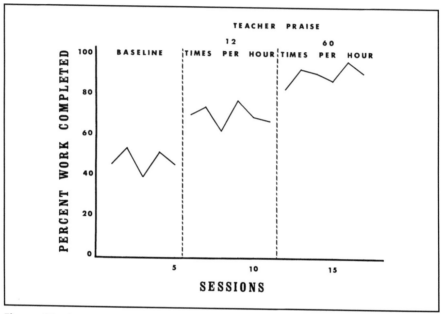

Figure 17. An example of the intensified treatments design. Following baseline a treatment that consists of a low frequency of teacher praise is introduced followed by a treatment that consists of a higher frequency of praise.

It is important to remember that this design works best when you introduce the treatment at only two or, at the most, three different intensities. If you use more intensities, the differences among performances under each condition tend to be small and the amount of overlap increases. This tends to obscure any changes and makes the data appear to show continuous improvement rather than change as the result of careful experimental control. The hypothetical data presented in Figure 18 compare the effects of using two or five treatment intensities on the degree of control demonstrated. The effect of introducing the treatment at too many intensities reduces the clarity of the degree of control demonstrated.

Table 2 lists the various behavior analysis research designs, gives some examples of how they are frequently used, and names the pros and cons associated with each design. It is often necessary to decide between several possible designs. Some designs can be ruled out because they are not at all suitable, but you may still be left with a choice between two or more options. When you have a choice, practical considerations such as effort, cost, and

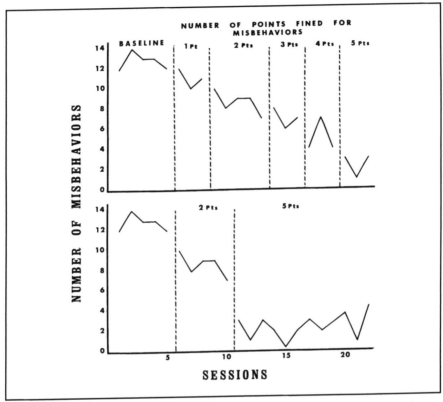

Figure 18. The results of an intensified tretment design with many treatment intensities (upper graph) and only two treatment intensities (lower graph).

how to make the most convincing presentation of the results take precedence in making the final decision.

Systematic Replication

Whenever several changes are made in replicating the effects of a particular experimental treatment, the process is termed a *systematic replication*. Systematic replications convey information on the range of conditions under which a particular experimental condition will be effective. Direct replication increases our confidence in the reliability of a finding. Systematic replication

(text continues on page 90)

Table 2
Pros and Cons of Various Research Designs

Research Design	Definition	Pros	Cons
Reversal	Following a baseline period a treatment is introduced, removed, and reintroduced.	Provides very convincing evidence that the treatment was responsible for the change in behavior. Can be used when the behavior of only one person is being studied.	The change in behavior may be relatively permanent and therefore not return to baseline levels when the treatment is removed. Return to baseline levels may be harmful to the client or others (ethical concerns).
Multiple Baseline Across Individuals or Groups	Baseline data are collected on the behavior of two or more persons or groups of persons. The treatment is then introduced for one person or group while the remaining person(s) or groups remain in the baseline condition. Once behavior has changed the treatment is introduced for another person or group, etc.	This design is effective when the effects of the treatment are not reversible or a reversal is contraindicated for ethical reasons.	Need to have more than one individual or group requiring the treatment.
Multiple Baseline Across Behaviors	Baseline data are collected on two or more behaviors of the same individual or group. The treatment is first introduced for one behavior and once that behavior has changed it is introduced for the next behavior, etc.	Can work when you have only one person or group with which to work.	Does not work when the behaviors tend to co-vary such as two types of aggression.

(continues)

Table 2 (*Continued*)

Research Design	Definition	Pros	Cons
Multiple Baseline Across Situations	Baseline data are collected on one behavior of an individual or group in two or more situations. The treatment is first introduced in one situation and once the behavior has changed is introduced in one of the remaining behaviors, etc.	Can work when you have only a single behavior of an individual or group.	Does not work if there is generalization from one situation to other situations. Generalization becomes more likely the more situations are treated.
Alternating Treatments	Following a baseline condition two treatments are introduced each day. The order of treatment introduction is randomly determined each day. This design results in two data paths (one for each treatment).	A good way to compare the effectiveness of two different treatments. It is a very powerful design because it controls for confounding variables.	Is not effective if treatment effects are not reversible.
Changing Criterion	Data are collected on one behavior of one person or group of people in one situation. Once the behavior has changed the criterion for the production of reinforcement is altered.	Can be effective when you have only one baseline for behavior for one person in one situation.	Less convincing than the reversal and multiple baseline designs.
Intensified Treatment	Data are collected on one behavior of one person or group of people in one situation. Once the behavior has changed the intensity of the treatment is increased.	Same as above.	Same as above.

also increases our confidence in its generality. Demonstrating that a particular experimental procedure will work with different types of individuals (e.g., older person or person with mental retardation) is one type of systematic replication. Demonstrating that it will work in another type of setting such as school, work, or home is also systematic replication. Finally, varying one of the treatment variables (e.g., the amount or type of reinforcement given) also extends the generality of findings.

Functional Analysis

Functional analysis is one type of behavioral assessment which makes use of replication-based design logic to determine why someone is engaging in a particular behavior. The information obtained from a functional analysis can be very useful in designing an effective treatment plan. In a functional analysis, one attempts to determine the cause of operant behavior in terms of its function. In other words, one identifies the reinforcer(s) maintaining the behavior. We also can use the research design logic to determine environmental stimuli that control or guide the behavior of interest.

The first step in a functional analysis is to examine the behavior using an ABC analysis. This will often give you hunches or hypotheses about what reinforcers are maintaining a behavior, as well as events that trigger the behavior. Next, we can use the experimental designs mentioned above to test our hunches in a relatively brief period of time. The data collected from the functional analysis then can be used to design an effective treatment plan.

The most common reasons that people engage in behavior is to produce positive reinforcers and to escape negative reinforcers. Examples of potential positive reinforcers are attention from a parent, teacher, employer, or peer; eating a tasty dinner; buying something you want, or having someone buy you something. Examples of potential negative reinforcers are being told you don't have to finish a job or task you don't like doing; getting a task you don't like doing postponed; arguing with someone rather than doing work you don't want to do; not wearing ear or eye protective equipment because it is uncomfortable; or getting out of a social obligation that makes you anxious.

Once you have a hunch about the potential reinforcers maintaining the behavior you wish to change, the next step is to test your hunch by alternating conditions that test your hunch. There are three ways to test your hunch. One way is to vary the motivation (establishing operations) for the suspected reinforcers. For example, if you think the behavior being engaged in is to obtain attention, you could examine how often the behavior occurs when lots of attention is provided versus when little attention is provided. If you think the behavior is maintained by escaping some task that is being taught, you can vary the difficulty of the task. The hypothesis is that the problem would occur more when the work is difficult than when it is easy. This can be tested by simply alternating 5-minute periods of hard and easy work and looking at how frequently the behavior occurs when the task is easy versus when it is difficult. Figure 19 shows how the results of such a comparison might look.

This type of analysis is similar to that used in a reversal design, with the exception that conditions are changed rapidly rather than over periods of days or weeks. This approach also has elements in common with an alternating treatments design, with numerous applications of the two conditions in a single day. Another type of functional analysis involves comparing a condition in which the behavior is reinforced whenever it occurs with a condition in which the suspected reinforcer occurs only when the behavior has not occurred for a short period of time. In other words, the suspected reinforcer is delivered only when the behavior is omitted. For example, if one suspects that the function of the behavior is to escape a task, you could compare doing

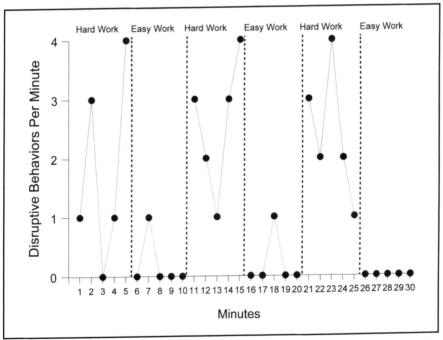

Figure 19. Rapidly switching between hard and easy work to determine whether the function of disruptive behavior is to escape.

some of the work for the student whenever the student engaged in the problem behavior versus doing some of the work for the student whenever the student engaged in good work-related behavior.

One can also perform a functional analysis by comparing having the suspected reinforcer follow the behavior with having it not follow the behavior (extinction). One weakness of this approach is that it takes time for extinction to take place, and it is therefore necessary to employ long experimental periods under the two conditions.

Replication logic designs can also be used to test other hunches you have. For example, in one study Van Houten (1993) found that a person with a developmental disability was slapping his face to receive sensory reinforcement. After performing a functional analysis which involved alternating 5-minute periods with a vibrator on and a vibrator off to determine whether the person was slapping his face to produce stimulation, a treatment was selected that involved having the person wear soft wrist weights. First, the treatment was tested by alternating 5-minute periods when the weights were on with 5-minute periods when the weights were off. The data collected in a 35-minute period (Figure 20) showed that face slapping increased after

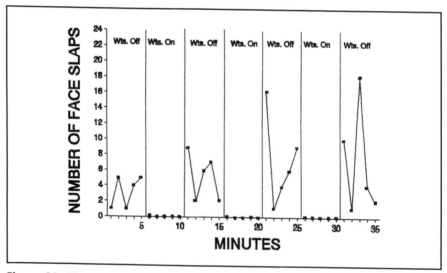

Figure 20. The number of face slaps per minute when wrist weights were on and when they were off. *Note.* From "The use of wrist weights to reduce self-injury maintained by sensory reinforcement," by R. Van Houten, 1993, *Journal of Applied Behavior Analysis, 26,* 197–203. Copyright 1993 by the Society for the Experimental Analysis of Behavior. Reprinted with permission.

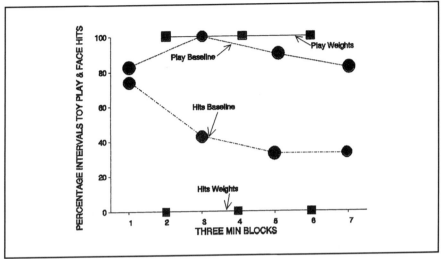

Figure 21. The percentage of intervals during which Tom hit his face and played with toys when he did or did not wear wrist weights. *Note.* From "The use of wrist weights to reduce self-injury maintained by sensory reinforcement," by R. Van Houten, 1993, *Journal of Applied Behavior Analysis, 26,* 197–203. Copyright 1993 by the Society for the Experimental Analysis of Behavior. Reprinted with permission.

the wrist weights were removed over each 5-minute test period, while face slapping was always zero when the weights were on.

Because the weights might also reduce appropriate behaviors, it was also necessary to examine what effect they had on toy play. The data presented in Figure 21 show that play was not adversely affected by wearing the weights. Abbreviated use of replication logic designs can be a useful tool for pretesting a variety of potential treatments as well as a way of detecting possible side effects.

Final Test

1. Give two good reasons why we should measure behavior.

   a. _____

   b. _____

(continues)

2. What are three standards a good behavioral definition should meet?

a. _____

b. _____

c. _____

3. Why is it important to select and define a behavior to increase when trying to decrease a behavior? _____

_____

4. What are five factors that can lead to poor interobserver agreement?

a. _____

b. _____

c. _____

d. _____

e. _____

5. What is automatic recording? _____

_____

_____

6. Give one good example of a behavior that can easily be automatically recorded.

_____

7. What is the direct measurement of lasting products? _____

_____

_____

(continues)

8. Give an example of a good permanent product measure. ______________

____

9. What is ABC recording and why is it important? ______________________

____

____

10. What are behavior counts? ______________________________________

____

____

11. Give examples of two behaviors that could be recorded with checklists.

    a. ____

    b. ____

12. Calculate the interobserver agreement between the two teachers' counts of the number of times a student talked out in the classroom.

    Observer 1 𝍸 𝍸 𝍸 //

    Observer 2 𝍸 𝍸 ////

    Interobserver agreement ________________

13. What are the four most useful types of observational recording?

    a. ____

    b. ____

    c. ____

    d. ____

(continues)

14. Define whole interval recording. _____

_____

_____

15. Define partial interval recording. _____

_____

_____

16. When should partial interval recording be employed?

a. _____

b. _____

17. Give an example of a latency measure. _____

_____

18. In the example below, two observers sampled whether a student was working every 20 minutes. Calculate the overall interobserver agreement and the interobserver agreement on the occurrence and nonoccurrence of the behavior.

OBSERVER 1

9:00	9:20	9:40
✓		✓
10:00	10:20	10:40
	✓	
11:00	11:20	11:40
✓		
12:00	12:20	12:40
✓	✓	
1:00	1:20	1:40
	✓	✓

OBSERVER 2

9:00	9:20	9:40
✓		
10:00	10:20	10:40
	✓	
11:00	11:20	11:40
✓		✓
12:00	12:20	12:40
✓	✓	
1:00	1:20	1:40
	✓	✓

(continues)

Overall interobserver agreement _____

Interobserver agreement on the occurrence _____

Interobserver agreement on the nonoccurrence _____

19. Why is it important when observing to disguise your interest in a child's behavior by varying the apparent object of your glances?

_____

20. What types of baselines are illustrated in the examples below?

a. _____

b. _____

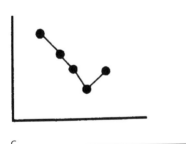

c. _____

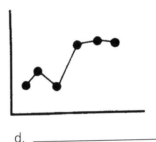

d. _____

21. How many phases or conditions are there in an AB Design? _____

22. Draw an example of a reversal design, labeling each of the conditions or phases.

(continues)

23. What are two factors that limit the use of reversal designs?

    a. _____

    b. _____

24. What is a multiple baseline design? _____

    _____

    _____

    _____

25. Name the four types of multiple baseline designs.

    a. _____   c. _____

    b. _____   d. _____

26. Sketch an example of a multiple baseline design.

27. What is the primary advantage of the multiple baseline design?

    _____

28. Describe the changing criterion design. _____

    _____

    _____

    _____

(continues)

29. When should the changing criterion design and the intensified treatment designs be chosen over a multiple baseline design?

_____

_____

30. For what is the alternating treatments design used? _____

_____

31. Sketch an example of an alternating treatments design. Be sure to label each graph.

32. What are the advantages of replication designs? _____

_____

_____

33. In the examples below, circle the results that are convincing demonstrations of the effectiveness of the treatment.

a.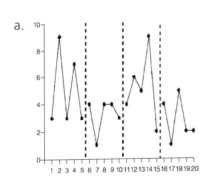

b.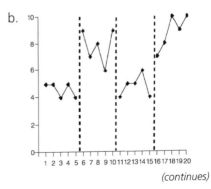

(continues)

c.

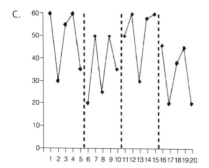

d.

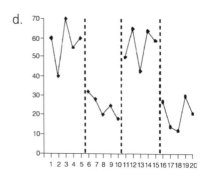

e.

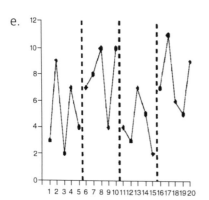

f.

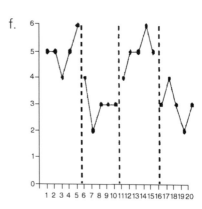

g.

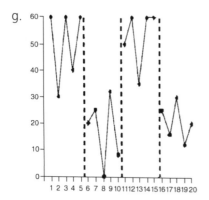

h.

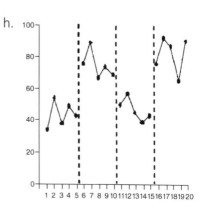

(continues)

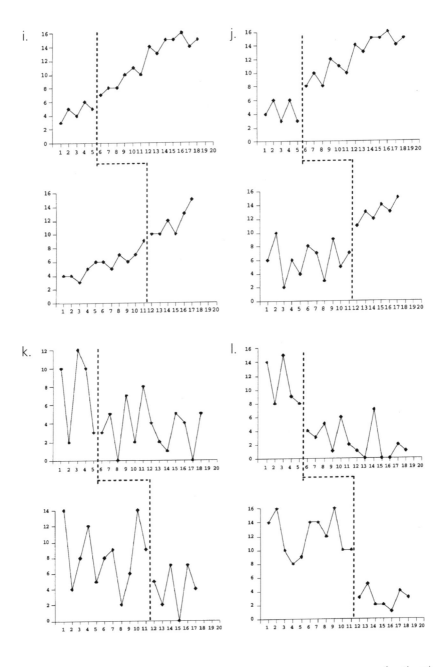

(continues)

m.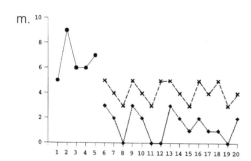

n.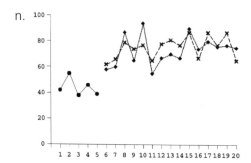

34. Give two reasons for conducting a functional analysis.

a. _____

b. _____

35. What is the first step in performing a functional analysis? _____

_____

_____

36. How does functional analysis differ from typical research designs?

_____

_____

Summary

The management of behavior involves a number of important steps. The first step is to define the behavior of interest in a precise way. This is done by writing down specific examples of behaviors or products of behaviors. These examples should be specific enough that anyone reading them would be able to pick out examples of the behaviors. Good definitions should be objective, clear, and complete.

The second step in the management of behavior is to select the most appropriate way to measure the carefully defined behavior of interest. The choice of method is dictated by the type of behavior you wish to measure and the resources you have available to measure it. Generally, automatic recording devices are most appropriate when the measuring devices are already available (e.g., time clocks, watt-hour meters, computers). Lasting products are most appropriate when the behavior of interest is some aspect of someone's output which leaves a record such as a completed test, damage to property, or the number of keyboarding errors per page.

Observational recording is employed when the behavior of interest cannot conveniently be recorded by a machine and leaves no permanent product. Four of the most useful methods of observational recording are behavior counts, checklists, duration recording, and time sampling. These measures provide information on how often a behavior occurs (behavior counts), whether or not the targeted behaviors occurred (checklists), how long it occurs (duration recording), and the percentage of the time the behavior occurs (time sampling). Other frequently used techniques are latency recording, whole interval recording, and partial interval recording.

Whenever permanent product or observational recording techniques are used, have a second scorer or observer record the behavior and calculate interscorer or interobserver agreement. Each observer should record the behavior at the same time and be unaware of what the other observer is recording. If interobserver agreement is not high it will likely be necessary to reexamine the definition, increase training, or redesign the recording sheet or observational protocol.

Once data have been obtained, each new point should be graphed as soon as it becomes available. A baseline or pretreatment measure should always be obtained to determine how much the behavior is occurring before any treatment or new program is tried. A good baseline can also show whether a behavior is increasing over time (ascending baseline), decreasing over time (descending baseline), or remaining about the same (level baseline). Baseline measures should continue until the type of baseline is clarified.

As a general rule, you can introduce a program designed to decrease a behavior if the behavior is level or increasing, and you can introduce a program to increase a behavior if the behavior is level or decreasing. Not only is it unwise to introduce a treatment when the data show a trend in the direction in which you want to produce a change, but also when the most recent data points suggest the beginning of such a trend. At the same time the measurement technique is being selected, it is important to select a research design because the type of design selected dictates the types and number of baselines obtained. It may also be helpful to perform a functional analysis prior to implementing a treatment to determine current reinforcers that are maintaining the behavior. It is also possible to perform an assessment to compare several potential treatments before selecting the final treatment. The importance of performing a functional analysis is most important when the behavior is serious.

Once a good baseline is obtained, the new program is introduced according to the selected research design. If it is not likely that the behavior change will be permanent and there is no ethical reason not to return to the original baseline, a reversal design can be employed. With this design a program or change is introduced after the first baseline period. Next, the program or change is removed and reintroduced to replicate the original results.

If the behavior change is permanent or if it would be unwise to return to the original conditions for ethical or political reasons, a multiple baseline design can be employed. With this design several baselines are obtained on different individuals, different groups, different behaviors, or the same behavior in different situations. The program is then introduced to each baseline successively.

If the purpose is to compare two or more different programs or procedures, the alternating treatments design is usually the best technique. With this design different programs are applied at different times each day. This design tends to reduce the influence of uncontrolled factors which cause day-to-day fluctuations in behavior. This is one reason why the alternating treatments design is so effective in comparing two or more treatment programs.

The changing criterion and intensified treatment designs demonstrate experimental control where it is not possible to use the reversal design and the presence of only one baseline precludes the use of a multiple baseline. With these designs either the criterion for reinforcement or the intensity of the treatment is increased over several steps. If the behavior changes in steps that correspond with the changes in the criterion or intensity of the treatment, experimental control is demonstrated.

Quiz Answers

Quiz 1

1. So different observers measure the same thing

2. a. objective,   b. clear,   c. complete

3. You should have mentioned specific behaviors that teachers are expected to do but that this teacher does not perform to standard. Examples of such behaviors are preparation of lesson plans, correction of papers on time, providing specific feedback when correcting papers, and so on. Note that all these behaviors are targets that you would like to increase.

4. To test the adequacy of the definition of the behavior and to test the reliability of the observer.

5. a. Whether the definition is sufficiently clear, complete, and objective.

   b. Whether the task is too complex (too many behaviors to score or recording sheet not well designed).

   c. Whether the observation period is too long.

   d. Whether the level of training is adequate.

   e. Whether the observers could be biased.

6. Answers will vary.

7. Answers will vary.

8. Answers will vary.

9. 83%

Quiz 2

1. The observer records behaviors of interest, noting what happened just before and just after the behavior occurred.

2. It can help identify situations associated with the behavior occurring as well as possible reinforcers that may be maintaining the behavior.

3. An observer records the number of times a behavior occurs during a particular period.

4. If the behavior is obvious, this form of recording does not interfere with ongoing tasks.

5. For possible responses, see Table 1.

6. a. Tally the behavior each time it occurs.

   b. Mark down the time the behavior occurs.

7. 86%

8. 93%

9. Recording how long a behavior occurs or lasts.

10. The average difference between the durations reported by the two observers.

11. Each observation session is divided into equal time periods or intervals. The behavior must persist throughout an entire interval to be scored for that interval.

12. When the behavior is one you would like the person to be engaging in most of the time.

13. The observation session is divided into equal time periods or intervals. The behavior is scored if it occurs at all during the interval.

14. a. When the behavior is one you would like to decrease.

    b. When the behavior is one which typically lasts for only a short time.

15. An observer records whether a behavior is occurring at the end of specified intervals.

16. a. When the observers don't have much time to record the behavior.

    b. When the behavior occurs reasonably often.

17. 80%

18. The behavior should fit into discrete categories such as: occurred vs. did not occur; correct vs. incorrect; completed vs. not completed, etc.

Quiz 3

1. a. Have the person in charge introduce you.

    b. Your entrance and departure should coincide with a natural break.

    c. Do not talk with other observers unless absolutely necessary.

    d. Do not talk to persons you are observing. Politely tell them you are busy and cannot talk.

    e. Disguise your interest by varying the apparent object of your glances.

2. The measurement of a behavior over a period of time in order to establish its level before introducing a program.

3. a. Example:

    b. Example: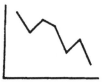

    c. Example:

4. a. No   b. Yes   c. Yes   d. Yes   e. No   f. Yes

Quiz 4

1. Median = 5   Mean = 5.1

2. Median = 7.5   Mean = 7.5

Final Test Answers

1. a. To evaluate programs.

    b. To provide performance feedback.

2. a. objective   b. clear   c. complete

3. Because it is easier to decrease a behavior when you are teaching a behavior to replace it, and it gives you a more positive basis for interacting with the person.

4. a. a poor definition

   b. too complex a task

   c. not enough training

   d. not enough breaks

   e. observer bias

5. Recording behavior or its products with a machine.

6. e.g., key punches on a computer, persons entering a ball park.

7. Measuring the lasting products of a behavior.

8. e.g., clothes left on floor.

9. Recording what happens before and after behaviors of interest. It can be helpful in identifying situations associated with the behavior and reinforcers maintaining the behavior.

10. An observer records the number of times a behavior occurs during a particular period.

11. For possible responses, see Table 1.

12. 82.4%

13. a. behavior or frequency counting

    b. checklists

    c. duration recording

    d. time sampling

14. Each observation session is divided into equal intervals. The behavior must persist throughout an entire interval to be scored for that interval.

15. Each observation session is divided into equal time intervals. The behavior is scored for an interval if it occurs at all during that interval.

16. a. When the behavior is one you would like to decrease.

    b. When the behavior is one which lasts for only a short time.

17. e.g., time elapsed from when breakfast is ready and a family sits at the table.

18. overall agreement 86.7%, agreement on occurrence 77.8%, agreement on nonoccurrence 75%

19. In order to not make the child feel uncomfortable.

20. a. ascending   b. level   c. descending   d. ascending

21. Two

22. For examples of these, see Figures 6 and 7.

23. a. Lack of reversibility

    b. When the behavior of interest is dangerous to the person studied or to others.

24. Design in which two or more baselines are recorded, then an experimental condition is introduced until a change is observed in the first baseline, and then successively in the second, third, and so on.

25. a. Across individuals

    b. Across groups

    c. Across behaviors

    d. Across situations

26. For examples of these, see Figures 8, 9, 10, 11, and 12.

27. The behavior change need not be reversible.

28. Following baseline, the criterion for performance is changed in stepwise fashion until the behavior meets the criterion level, whereupon the criterion is changed to the next step, and so on.

29. When you have only one baseline available.

30. To compare the effects of two or more treatments or conditions.

31. For examples of these, see Figures 13, 14, and 15.

32. The effects of a variable can be quickly evaluated. Replication designs: don't require random assignment of people to conditions; don't require a large number of participants; allow all participants to receive treatment; allow the researcher to determine which participants responded to the treatment; allow the researcher to make changes to the treatment if it does not produce the desired change in behavior.

33. You should have circled b; d; f; g; h; j; l; and m.

34. a. identify reinforcers maintaining the behavior

    b. identify stimuli associated with the problem behavior

35. The first step in performing a functional analysis is to generate good hunches about what is reinforcing the behavior.

36. Conditions typically applied for only a short period of time with functional analysis designs.

References and Further Reading

Baer, D. M. (1977). Perhaps it would be better not to know everything. *Journal of Applied Behavior Analysis, 10*, 167–172.

Cooper, J. O. (1981). *Measuring behavior.* Columbus, OH: Merrill.

Critchfield, T. S. (1999). An unexpected effect of recording frequency in reactive self-monitoring. *Journal of Applied Behavior Analysis, 32*, 389–391.

Day, H. M., Horner, R. H., & O'Neill, R. E. (1994). Multiple functions of problem behaviors: Assessment and intervention. *Journal of Applied Behavior Analysis, 27*, 270–289.

Goetz, E., & Baer, D. M. (1971). Social reinforcement of "creative" block building by young children. In E. A. Ramp & B. L. Hopkins (Eds.), *A new direction in education: Behavior analysis* (pp. 72–79). Lawrence: University of Kansas.

Goetz, E. M., & Salmonson, M. M. (1972). The effect of general and descriptive reinforcement on creativity in easel painting. In G. B. Semb (Ed.), *Behavior analysis in education* (pp. 53–61). Lawrence: University of Kansas.

Greenwood, C. R., Delquadri, J. C., & Hall, R. V. (1984). Opportunity to respond and student academic performance. In W. L. Heward, T. E. Heron, D. S. Hill, & J. Trap-Porter (Eds.), *Focus on behavior analysis in education* (pp. 58–88). Columbus, OH: Merrill.

Hall, R. V. (1971, April). Training teachers in classroom use of contingency management. *Educational Technology, 11*, 33–38.

Hall, R. V., Axelrod, S., Foundopoulos, M., Shellman, J., Campbell, R. A., & Cranston, S. S. (1971). The effective use of punishment to modify behavior in the classroom. *Educational Technology, 11*, 24–26.

Hall, R. V., Cristler, C., Cranston, S., & Tucker, B. (1970). Teachers and parents as researchers using multiple-baseline designs. *Journal of Applied Behavior Analysis, 3*, 247–255.

Hall, R. V., & Fox, R. G. (1977). Changing criterion designs: An alternative applied behavior analysis procedure. In B. C. Etzel, J. M. Le Blanc, & D. M. Baer (Eds.), *New developments in behavioral research, theory, method and application.* Hillsdale, NJ: Erlbaum.

Hall, R. V., Fox, R., Willard, D., Goldsmith, L., Emerson, M., Owen, M., David F., & Porcia, E. (1971). The teacher as observer and experimenter in the modification of disputing and talking out behaviors. *Journal of Applied Behavior Analysis, 4*, 141–149.

Hall, R. V., Lund, D., & Jackson, D. (1968). Effects of teacher attention on study behavior. *Journal of Applied Behavior Analysis, 1*, 1–12.

Hersen, M., & Barlow, D. H. (1976). *Single case experimental designs: Strategies for studying behavior change.* New York: Pergamon Press.

Horner, R. H., Day H. M., & Day J. R. (1997). Using neutralizing routines to reduce problem behaviors. *Journal of Applied Behavior Analysis, 30*, 601–614.

Kahng, S. W., & Iwata, B. A. (1999). Correspondence between outcomes of brief and extended functional analysis. *Journal of Applied Behavior Analysis, 32*, 149–159.

Kazdin, A. E. (1980). *Research design in clinical psychology.* New York: Harper & Row.

Kazdin, A. E. (2000). *Behavior modification in applied settings* (6th ed.). New York: Brooks/Cole.

Kazdin, A. E., & Geesey, S. (1977). Simultaneous treatments design. *Behavior Therapy, 8,* 682–693.

Larson, L. D., Schnelle, J. F., Kirchner, R. E., Carr, A. F., Domash, M. A., & Risley, T. R. (1980). Reduction of police vehicle accidents through mechanically aided supervision. *Journal of Applied Behavior Analysis, 13,* 571–582.

Malenfant, J. E. L., & Van Houten, R. (1989). Increasing the percentage of drivers yielding to pedestrians in Canadian cities with a multifaceted safety program. *Health Education Research Theory and Practice, 5,* 275–279.

Malenfant, L., Wells, J. K., Van Houten, R., & Williams, A. F. (1996). The use of feedback to increase observed daytime seat belt use in two cities in North Carolina. *Accident Analysis and Prevention, 28,* 771–777.

Rapp, J. T., Milternberger, R. G., Galensky, T. L., Ellingson, S. A., & Long, E. S. (1999). A functional analysis of hair pulling. *Journal of Applied Bahavior Analysis, 32,* 329–337.

Retting, R. A., & Van Houten, R. (2000). Safety benefits of advance stop lines at signalized intersections: Results of a field evaluation. *ITE Journal, 70,* 47–54.

Richman, D. M., Wacker, D. P., Asmus, J. M., Casey, S. D., & Andelman, M. (1999). Further analysis of problem behavior in response class hierarchies. *Journal of Applied Behavior Analysis, 32,* 269–283.

Risley, T. R. (1971). Spontaneous language in the preschool environment. In Julian Stanley (Ed.), *Research on curriculums for preschools.* Baltimore: Johns Hopkins.

Sidman, M. (1960). *Tactics of scientific research.* New York: Basic.

Skinner, B. R. (1953). *Science and human behavior.* New York: MacMillan.

Skinner, C. H., Cooper, L., & Cole, C. L. (1997). The effects of oral presentation previewing rates on reading performance. *Journal of Applied Behavior Analysis, 30,* 331–333.

Sulzer-Azaroff, B., & Mayer, G. R. (1977). *Applying behavior-analysis procedures with children and youth.* New York: Holt, Rinehart & Winston.

Van Houten, R. (1993). The use of wrist weights to reduce self-injury maintained by sensory reinforcement. *Journal of Applied Behavior Analysis, 26,* 197–203.

Van Houten, R., & Malenfant, L. (1992). The influence of signs prompting motorists to yield 50 feet (15.5 m) before marked crosswalks on motor vehicle-pedestrian conflicts at crosswalks with pedestrian activated flashing lights. *Accident Analysis and Prevention, 24,* 217–225.

Van Houten, R., Nau, P. A., Mackenzie-Keating, S. E., Sameoto, D., & Colavecchia, B. (1982). An analysis of some variables influencing the effectiveness of reprimands. *Journal of Applied Behavior Analysis, 15,* 65–83.

Van Houten, R., Retting, R. A., Van Houten, J., Farmer, C. M., & Malenfant, J. E. L. (1999). The use of animation in LED pedestrian signals to improve pedestrian safety. *ITE Journal, 69,* 30–38.

Wolf, M., Risley, T., & Mees, H. (1964). Application of operant conditioning procedures to the behavior problems of an autistic child. *Behaviour Research and Therapy, 1,* 305–312.

About the Authors

Ron Van Houten, PhD, is professor of psychology at Mount Saint Vincent University, Halifax, Nova Scotia. He has published over 100 articles and books in the area of applied behavior analysis and has been widely recognized for the behavioral research he has carried out in classrooms, homes, and the community. Dr. Van Houten has experience applying behavior analysis measurement and research designs to solve problems in a wide variety of situations, ranging from classroom and clinical interventions to traffic safety in the community.

R. Vance Hall, PhD, is senior scientist emeritus of the Bureau of Child Research and professor emeritus of Human Development and Family Life and Special Education at the University of Kansas. He was a pioneer in carrying out behavioral research in classrooms and in homes.